The Classical Age of

GERMAN LITERATURE

The Classical Age of
GERMAN LITERATURE
1748 – 1805

By

L. A. WILLOUGHBY, M.A., D.Lit., Ph.D.

Professor Emeritus in the University of London

NEW YORK / RUSSELL & RUSSELL

1966

FIRST PUBLISHED IN 1926
REISSUED, 1966, BY RUSSELL & RUSSELL
A DIVISION OF ATHENEUM HOUSE, INC.
BY ARRANGEMENT WITH OXFORD UNIVERSITY PRESS
L. C. CATALOG CARD NO: 66—15438

PRINTED IN THE UNITED STATES OF AMERICA

PREFACE

IN writing this book I had in view especially two types of reader : the general public for whom this series is intended, and the young student of German literature, whether he be in his last year at school or his first year at college. I have tried to compose a connected story in which the main lines should not be obscured by the mass of detail. In thus simplifying the picture I am conscious of having somewhat destroyed the perspective. The early Romantic School, for instance, was in many ways complementary and parallel to the classical movement, and it was also largely contemporaneous. But it is so big with new problems and theories that it could only find adequate treatment in a separate volume. Again, it may seem arbitrary to break off the narrative with the death of Schiller. But 1805 is a convenient date which at least marks the apogee of the movement, just as its beginnings must be sought in the attempts of Gottsched to organize literature on the basis of Wolffian rationalism.

This book aims at presenting German letters not merely as a national product, but also as the reflection of inter-national thought in the cosmopolitan eighteenth century. As such it may prove of interest to the student of comparative literature. I have naturally endeavoured to incorporate the results of recent research, both English and foreign, and some of my obligations (though by no means all) are recorded in the 'Select Bibliography'. The latter, I feel, is especially open to criticism ; it is bound to contain either too much

or too little ; the books quoted are of unequal value ; many
of them may appear very special.   But I trust that in its
international aspect it may prove useful to the student
anxious to view German literature from as many different
angles as possible.

It is now more than twenty years ago since I sat at the
feet of Professor J. G. Robertson and heard for the first
time most of the names which appear in the following pages.
This little sketch will testify to the keen interest which his
lectures aroused.   It owes still more to the ripe scholarship
of his numerous writings, and it has profited especially by
his careful and sympathetic reading of the proofs.   At the
same time I alone must be held responsible for the book's
shortcomings, and for any errors of fact or judgement.   To
Mr. C. T. Onions, Fellow of Magdalen College, the general
editor, are due my grateful thanks, not only for including
this book in his series, but also for numerous and valuable
suggestions made both while it was in manuscript and in
proof.

L. A. WILLOUGHBY.

SHEFFIELD,
November, 1925.

CONTENTS

I

THE PREMISES

ANY dispassionate observer taking up a history of German literature will be struck first of all by its comparative paucity ; three quarters of the volume, he will find, are devoted to German letters since the second half of the eighteenth century, and he will seek in vain for any traces of such epochs of literary splendour as our own Elizabethan period or the age of Louis XIV. Germany came into its literary inheritance later than any other nation of Western Europe and modern German literature may be said only to have begun with the second half of the eighteenth century.

The causes of this backwardness are to be found less in any inherent defect of the German mind than in the outward circumstances which have governed German political and social life since the beginning of modern times. The sixteenth century was for Germany a century of splendid promise, in which it lagged behind its neighbours neither intellectually nor artistically. Humanism had met with an enthusiastic reception at the hands of German scholars, who responded nobly to its new ideals of life and art. Melanchthon and Reuchlin enjoyed a European reputation. Artistically the Renaissance found perfect expression in the works of Albrecht Dürer and Adam Krafft, and the castle of Heidelberg is one of the supreme monuments of Renaissance architecture. Spiritually, Germany was in the vanguard of progress : the Reformation, the movement which changed the aspect of the world, was the work of one of its greatest sons. In the world of science it could boast a Kepler, the man who revolutionized astronomy. Literature alone seemed untouched by the intense intellectual and artistic activity apparent everywhere else. Not that Germany was devoid of literary talent ; the mention of Brant, Hans Sachs, or Fischart, is sufficient to disprove this ; and we have the popular element at its best in the magnificent sincerity of the *Volkslied*. But what was needed was the direction of such talent towards a high ideal. Such an ideal might have been found in the religious aspects of the Reformation. But Luther was a reformer first and a poet afterwards, and fine as are his hymns, and monumental as is his great translation of the Bible, these are the accidental results of his plans of church reform, rather than the product of a set literary purpose. Militant protestantism was, if anything, detrimental to literature and gave too much prominence to personal satire and coarse invective. There was also lacking a strong national spirit, the consciousness of intellectual and political strength, such as existed in England and produced the wealth of Elizabethan poetry. Germany, by its geographical position, was cut off from any share in the inspiring achievements of the seafaring countries of the West. While France and England were being welded into great political unities under the strong personal rule of Francis I and of the Tudors, Germany fell under the sway of a foreigner who was ignorant of the very language of his new subjects. Far from uniting Germany into a great national whole, Charles V sought only to exploit the country for his personal ambitions. He opposed the national movement of the Reformation with all the moral and political power at his command and plunged the country into civil war. For the next hundred years Germany was split into two hostile camps, the Catholics who sought support, moral and financial, from Italy, and the Protestants who found it in treaties of alliance with the French king. This policy was to lead eventually to the cataclysm of the Thirty Years War, which completed the general disintegration of German life and art.

There are wars from which nations have emerged strengthened and exalted, but the Thirty Years War (1618–48) brought nothing but shameful humiliation. It was without fixed purpose and devoid of enthusiasm and patriotism ; the religious ideals receded more and more into the background, and it degenerated into a defensive alliance of the feudal states against the overweening pretensions of Austria to territorial supremacy. It had become a purely selfish war of private and dynastic interests, and it was waged almost entirely with foreign mercenaries, whose only thought was plunder. The condition of Germany at the Peace of Westphalia in 1648 was heartrending. Great tracts of fertile land had passed to foreign states ; the whole country was devastated and depopulated ; in the villages there was often not a wagon, not a domestic animal to be seen, and the peasant, to till his land, was forced to harness himself to the plough. Many of the great free cities of the Empire never recovered their former prosperity ; their trade was ruined and with it their position as art centres. Morality was at its lowest, for manners had suffered terribly under the excesses of a licentious soldiery. Everywhere was grossness, superstition, and injustice. The *Simplicissimus* of Grimmelshausen presents a pitiful picture of the general demoralization induced by the war.

The far-reaching and permanent consequences of the war were even more pernicious than the war itself. The imperial house was humbled, and, though the dangers which had threatened Germany from the revival of the dynastic aspirations of the Hapsburgs were averted, the might and unity of the Empire had gone for ever. Henceforth the Holy Roman Empire was a mere phantom state, in which the territorial princes were all-powerful, and the Emperor's authority little more than an empty name. Germany became the geographical designation for some 360 separate and practically independent states. Although Austria was nominally supreme, yet the influence of foreign powers like France or Sweden was of greater account in German politics. The history of Germany in the second half of the seventeenth century is the story of French aggressions and conquests. And worse still, with the outward power there disappeared also the last vestige of German patriotism. There existed no consciousness of nationality, and even a good German like Leibniz could look up to Louis XIV as a second Charlemagne, destined to protect the empire from the selfish policy of Austria and the ever increasing encroachments of the Turks. The loss of Alsace, of Toul and Verdun to France awakened nowhere any sense of dishonour and shame.

The pretensions of the territorial princes rose in proportion as the power of the emperor declined. Duke John Frederick of Hanover was but voicing the general opinion when he declared openly, ' I am the Emperor in my country ! ' Every independent prince, however small his state, assumed the same sovereign privileges. The absolutism of Louis XIV served as a model to every petty German Landgrave. The state and the subject were held to be the personal property of the sovereign, who ruled by divine right. Some German princes there were who, like Frederick the Great, the Emperor Joseph II, or Karl August of Weimar, considered themselves as ' the first servants of the state ' ; but the vast majority were petty tyrants like Karl Eugen of Wirtemberg, under whom Schubart and Schiller suffered, or like that Elector of Saxony who shot a slater from the roof of his palace merely to gratify a whim of his mistress. The shameful traffic in human cannon-fodder was common to most of the German princes of the day, and they sold their subjects impartially to Holland or England. Schiller's father, as recruiting officer to the Duke of Wirtemberg, must have pressed many a man into his master's service ; and to Schiller himself we owe a most realistic description in *Kabale und Liebe*. J. G. Seume (1763–1810), himself a victim, has left an account of his experiences as an involuntary soldier in America in *Aus meinem Leben* (1813).

In France the absolute monarchy was at least patriotic and national ; it was the munificent patron of art and literature, and under its aegis there arose the great French classics to testify to the splendour of the age. But in Germany, although the people suffered the same wrongs and oppression as in France, there was lacking the redeeming feature of great aims and great conditions—on the one hand the most unbounded despotism, on the other abject servility and time-serving. The life at the average German court was a shame to civilization, and no less shameful were the grovelling and flattery of the subjects. The composer Mattheson, in his dedication to Landgraf Ernst Ludwig of Hessen, surpasses himself in blasphemous adulation : ' If God did not exist, who could more fittingly take His place than Your Serene Highness ? '

The nobility had sunk to the same imitation of French extravagance. It had almost ceased to be German in its aping of French dress and manners. An exclusive aristocracy arose which looked down in contempt on the middle and lower classes. They were disdained as the ' canaille ', inter-marriage with them was a ' mésalliance ' (witness the plot of *Kabale und Liebe*) ; they were a different and lower order of beings (even Goethe's Werther as a commoner suffers under aristocratic arrogance). The result was an ever increasing desire to belong to the privileged class. Side by side with the old nobility of birth there arose a new nobility, the ' Briefadel ', conferred by letters patent, which might be bought for a moderate sum. And not the nobility alone, but every class of society was actuated by a mad desire of being better than that immediately below. It is the beginning of that extravagant love of titles which still, in spite of the Republic, excites the ridicule of the foreign traveller in Germany.

An immediate consequence of the flattery and adulation reigning on all hands was a change in the style of address. Along with French manners came the bombastic expressions of French classicism. Conversation in the best circles consisted of high-flown and unmerited compliments, as unnatural as they were exaggerated. The German never fully absorbed French culture ; he was by nature an honest, sentimental, deep-feeling individual. The stiffness and elaborate artificiality of the new manners accorded but ill with his natural simplicity ; he was lacking in all the graces of deportment and speech which sat so well on the Frenchman. And so his adoption of French culture was purely external and artificial, it consisted mainly in the conformity to strict rules and conventions which he had only imperfectly assimilated.

As in manners, so too in literature ; German works of the seventeenth and early eighteenth centuries are characterized by the conventionality and artificiality which obsessed the life and thought of the age. Such are the productions of the Second Silesian School, of Hofmannswaldau (1617–79) and Lohenstein (1635–83). Their works were crude, bombastic, rhetorical, whether they dealt in the drama or the novel. The ' galant ' French novel especially was much in vogue and did much to vitiate the taste and the morals of its German imitators.

The opponents of the Silesian School, the group of North German poets, the school of ' Hofpoeten ' at the magnificent and dissolute court of the Elector of Saxony, were but little

superior to the men they affected to despise. Such were
Rudolf von Canitz (1654–99), Benjamin Neukirch (1665–
1729), Johann von Besser (1654–1729), J. U. von König
(1688–1744), J. V. Pietsch (1690–1733), whose chief claim
to fame is as the butt of Frederick the Great's sarcasm. All
these poets were of mediocre talent, without inspiration,
hampered and dulled by slavish observance of the rules which
Boileau had expounded in his *Art poétique*. In this wilder-
ness the purer notes of a Christian Günther (1695–1723) or
of a Friedrich von Hagedorn (1708–54) could hardly make
themselves heard. Both France and England could look
back with pride on a great literary past, but Germany at the
beginning of the eighteenth century had not yet emerged
from the tentative imitations of the Renaissance. Both
politically and intellectually it was negligible, and the French
Jesuit Bouhours could, in 1671, formulate in all seriousness
the question whether a German might under any circumstances possibly have ' esprit '.

Nor was this patronizing contempt with which the chief
nation of Europe looked down on German culture un-
warranted when we realize that down to the middle of the
eighteenth century Germany was without even a uniform
language in which to express itself. While Latin remained
the language of schools and universities—the first German
lecture was not delivered until 1687—French became the
chief vehicle of intercourse for the nobility and gentry, and
French culture and fashions followed in its wake, not to be
displaced for another 150 years. At a time when the
languages of France and England had attained to a high state
of perfection through the common achievement of men of
letters and scholars centred round the court and the capital,
Germany unhappily knew no such unifying tendencies. In
spite of the Lutheran Bible, north and south still clung

obstinately each to its own idiom, and the German literary language had still to be fashioned. The early works of Wieland, Goethe, and Schiller are tinged by their southern dialects, and, under their influence, rhymes peculiar to the dialects of the south were allowed to pass muster throughout the classical period. Leibniz (1646–1716), for all his enthusiasm for his mother tongue, found it so unsuited for the expression of abstract thought that he chose to write his chief works in French. Frederick the Great, with all his patriotism, spoke German 'like a coachman', and as late as 1780 wrote a pamphlet on German literature in French. For three years Berlin, under Voltaire, became the centre of French culture ; the Berlin Academy was modelled entirely on the Parisian pattern ; a Frenchman was its president and its transactions were carried on in French. During the seventeenth and eighteenth centuries no fewer than 2,000 French words were absorbed into the language, and German was rapidly on the way to become a mixed language like English. But about the middle of the eighteenth century a reaction took place, and Wolff's chief claim to fame is less as the pioneer of rationalism than as the creator of a German philosophical language which prepared the way for Kant to write his native tongue. Lessing had first to create the vehicle for his criticism—for a moment he seriously considered recasting the *Laokoon* in French. Goethe himself was brought up in a French atmosphere and in his youth had a certain predilection for French correspondence ; the works written in Leipzig, though German in language, are still entirely French in feeling. From this time onwards the process of creating artificially a German literary language has proceeded uninterruptedly, every great writer adding his quota, until in true German fashion the movement was finally organized by the ' Deutscher Sprachverein '.

II

THE AWAKENING

Though the weakness of German literature at the end of the seventeenth century was due primarily to an excessive imitation of foreign models, yet it owed its eventual salvation to similar external influences. It was English literature that was destined to inspire German letters to reach undreamed-of heights of excellence : from aristocratic France Germany turned for inspiration to democratic England. A silent social and economic revolution had in fact been slowly preparing itself in Germany. Since the beginning of the eighteenth century the loss of population occasioned by the Thirty Years War was being gradually made good, and by the middle of the century Berlin, for instance, had practically doubled its size. With the increase in population came increase in productivity and trade ; wealth became more evenly distributed, and a new middle class arose, which found leisure for education and culture. Where in the former generation literature was the preserve of courts and princes, it now found a more congenial background in the great commercial cities of the north,—in Hamburg, Leipzig, Berlin, which, with the ever-increasing importance of sea-traffic, had gradually superseded the old centres of land trade such as Nuremberg or Augsburg. And German authors were no longer recruited from court circles—all the great poets of the eighteenth century were of humble extraction. Goethe was the grandson of a tailor, Schiller's mother a baker's daughter, and others, like Lessing, Wieland, Schubart, Bürger, Herder, Kant, were all ' gut bürgerlich ', the sons of pastors, schoolmasters, and other petty government officials.

Many, it is true, passed their lives at the courts of princes, but the relations were mainly external ; it was the bourgeois element imposing itself on the court rather than the reverse.

English literary influence during the eighteenth century may conveniently be grouped in three stages : the first that of Addison, Pope, and Thomson, who are themselves largely the reflection of the French classical spirit. The chief exponent was Gottsched at Leipzig during the years 1720–40. The second stage, of Milton and Young, represented the religious and emotional side of literature, advocated so strongly by Bodmer at Zürich between 1740–60. The third was the strongest wave of all, bearing Shakespeare, Ossian, and Percy upon its crest, and first introducing to the Germans genius, originality, and spontaneity. The twenty years from 1760–80 were thus the most fertile in German literature and inaugurate that short but brilliant period during which Germany asserted its independence of foreign models, and, for the first time in history, assumed the leadership of European letters.

It is an axiom in modern German literary history that every new intellectual phase is heralded by an intense theoretical preparation. The German mind, with characteristic thoroughness, needs to be sure of its ground before it can build. Just as Opitz, some hundred years before, had endeavoured, by his theoretical essays, to lay the foundation of the new Renaissance poetry, so now Gottsched took up the work where it had been abandoned by his predecessor. Like Opitz, Gottsched (1700–66) conceived the idea of reforming German literature by constant reference to French models. But French literature had taken great strides in the meantime, and Gottsched's models were not the ' Pléiade ', but the great achievements of the age of Louis XIV. He saw in the French the acme of literary criticism (he owed more to D'Aubignac and Le Bossu than to Boileau), but he applied their rules with little appreciation of their deeper meaning. Fidelity to nature meant for him conformity with actuality and homely common sense. Correctness of diction was to be obtained by the sacrifice of imagination and colour.

These principles Gottsched enunciated with great effect in his *Versuch einer kritischen Dichtkunst für die Deutschen* 1730. The fact that they were strictly in keeping with the general mediocrity of the age assured the book's success, and Gottsched soon found himself the supreme arbiter of German literary taste. As professor of poetry at the university of Leipzig, the most fashionable of German universities, and the editor of several periodicals, his influence extended far beyond the confines of Germany, and his *Deutsche Sprachkunst* (1748) was translated into some of the chief European languages. In spite of his restricted talents, perhaps even because of them, it must be admitted that Gottsched wielded his powers wisely and well. The ' Deutschübende Gesellschaft ', which he refounded, could not, indeed, hope to rival its model, the Académie Française, but it at least prepared fertile ground for the literary seed he had to sow, and by insisting upon the dialect of Saxony, ' das Meissner Deutsch ', as the only correct form of literary German, he ensured the final victory of the Middle German idiom, which Luther and Opitz had already rendered predominant.

Gottsched's chief merit lies, however, in his purification of the theatre. He found the German stage occupied by little else than the farce and the ' Haupt- und Staatsaktionen ', the crude bombastic melodrama bequeathed by the English strolling players of the seventeenth century. Upon these he waged ceaseless war and he solemnly banished ' Hans Wurst ', or the fool, from the stage. He realized, too, that the crying need of the theatre was an adequate repertory of plays, and,

as these were entirely lacking in German, he set himself,
with the help of his wife and friends, to produce them by
translations from the French classical drama. The *Deutsche
Schaubühne* in six volumes, published between 1740–5, is
a collection of thirty-seven plays including a dozen by the
chief French authors. Gottsched even felt himself called
upon to write an uninspired tragedy of his own, *Der sterbende
Cato* (1732), which, however, is nothing but the amalgama-
tion of two plays by Deschamps and Addison.

Poor and indifferent though Gottsched's taste may have
been, mistaken as was his view of literature, his efforts at
least had the result of once more uniting literature and the
stage, which in Germany had never been in such close touch
before. But his reforms culminated in an even more important result, the definite predominance of the French
drama. For the next forty years the influence of the ' tragédie
classique' with its three unities, its principle of 'ideale Ferne'
(the remoteness of subject-matter or events), with its ' belle
et noble passion ', and, above all, with its dogma that only
great personages such as kings and princes were fit subjects
for the drama, is visible throughout the German drama of
the eighteenth century, down even to Goethe and Schiller.
And not all the dialectics of a Lessing, or the strictures of
a Wilhelm Schlegel, have been able to dethrone it from the
proud position of superiority which it still occupies in the
Germany of to-day.

Gottsched enjoyed his supremacy for ten years ; but his
conceit and pedantry were bound to arouse enmity. Formid-
able opponents arose in two Zürich professors, Bodmer
and Breitinger, the latter of whom capped Gottsched's
Kritische Dichtkunst with one of his own (1740). Not
that their critical standpoint could be termed a great advance
on that of Gottsched ; but they at least entered a plea for

metaphor and colour in poetry, advocated greater freedom of versification, and, above all, urged the importance of imagination as opposed to reason. Their theory was drawn partly from Addison and Du Bos, but chiefly from the Italian Muratori, and Milton was their justification; *Paradise Lost* had, in fact, been translated into prose by Bodmer as early as 1732, and his defence of its miraculous and supernatural elements excited Gottsched's wrath, and was the chief cause of the celebrated feud between the rival critics. Thus began that conflict between French and English taste which lasted during the whole of the century and in which Lessing was to play so important a part.

With forces so unequal—for the Swiss were justified by no less a personality than Albrecht von Haller (1708-77), the poet and world-famous physiologist—the issue could not be doubtful. When Klopstock, the avowed pupil of Bodmer, took the German world by storm with his *Messias*, Gottsched's fate was sealed. Henceforth he was left with but the shadow of a reputation, he was nothing but a pathetic quixotic figure of the past, who had attempted a task beyond his powers : ' He is despised by everybody, no one will associate with him ', Goethe wrote of him some twenty years later. The tragedy of Gottsched was that he lived to see the theories and the men he had combated bring forth a great harvest.

Tired of Gottsched's dictatorial methods, a group of young Leipzig students, formerly his disciples, now seceded from him. That they might give full vent to their opinion they founded a new journal, the *Neue Beiträge zum Vergnügen des Verstandes und Witzes* (1744-8), which, from the place of its publication, is famous in German literature as the *Bremer Beiträge*. It was in its pages that the first three cantos of Klopstock's *Messias* were published in 1748.

To-day the *Messias* hardly possesses more than an historical
interest ; it is impossible to read with enjoyment the nineteen
thousand or more hexameters which go to make up this
interminable epic.   And Klopstock failed where his model
Milton succeeded, because his method was wrong.   Not only
was his subject-matter unduly restricted—it comprises the
biblical narrative from Christ's ascent of the Mount of Olives
until His Ascension—but his treatment is lyric rather than
epic.   Out of pietistic reverence for the Redeemer, Klopstock
fails to render Him humanly interesting ; he neglects external
action for inward emotion, and wallows in sentimental effusions : ' The work is so full of feeling ', wrote Lessing most
aptly, ' that the reader feels nothing at all '.   The later cantos
are nothing but pious meditations, prayers, and hymns of
praise.   To us the theme of *Messias*, perhaps because of the
associations of Händel's *Messiah* (1741), suggests an oratorio
rather than an epic, but judged by contemporary standards it
was a great work of literature.   For the first time since the
Middle Ages a poet had arisen in Germany who was born
and not made, who was filled with the holy enthusiasm of his
office and knew how to express his lofty aspirations without
bombast.   In language, too, Klopstock was an innovator and,
through his careful choice of noble and euphonious expressions, his bold imagery and happy word-formations, may be
said to have created the poetic diction of Germany.

Although we no longer share the raptures of his contemporaries over the work of the German Milton, we can
still appreciate Klopstock's lyrical gifts, which appear at their
best in his *Oden* (1771).   With Horace as his model, he
eventually developed the free rhythm which Goethe later
was to bring to such perfection.   Klopstock also fell under
the spell of ' poor moaning, monotonous Macpherson ', and
was indirectly responsible for the subsequent Ossian fever in

Germany. And as the eighteenth century had not yet learnt
to differentiate between Celt and Teuton, Ossian became
for Klopstock and his successors the type of the national poet
of the Germanic past. To add to the confusion, Klopstock
ascribed the northern mythology of the *Edda* to all German
tribes without distinction: led astray by a passage in Tacitus,
he connected these mythical German poets with the Celtic
' bards ', and imagined them dwelling in sacred groves and
performing patriotic songs to the sound of the harp. In
his ode *Der Hügel und der Hain* he gave this thought poetic
form, ' Der Hügel ' being the German for Helicon, and
' Der Hain ' a symbol of patriotic poetry.

These patriotic aspirations found more complete expression
in his trilogy on Hermann, the Arminius of the Romans, and
prompted a crowd of second-rate imitators. Yet in a sense
Klopstock may be deemed to have awakened the national
consciousness of the Germans.

Apart from the *Messias*, Klopstock's deep religious feeling
also found expression in his *Geistliche Lieder* (1758 and 1769),
and especially in his biblical dramas *Der Tod Adams* (1757),
Salomo (1764), and *David* (1772). They are dreary reading,
but are so far of interest as they inspired the imitations of
both Goethe and Schiller. Goethe's *Belsazar* was almost
his earliest production, and Schiller in his earlier years produced a rival *Christ*, which, however, has entirely perished.
On the other hand the Zürich landscape-painter and poet,
Salomon Gessner, was fired by Klopstock's example to write
his *Tod Abels* (1758). Of greater importance are Gessner's
famous *Idyllen* (1756 and 1772), a continuation of the pastoral
literature of the seventeenth century, which became the most
popular book in Europe until Goethe's *Werther* contended
with it for the first place.

Although temporarily removed by Klopstock to Copenhagen, and then to Hamburg, the centre of German literature was to remain fixed in Leipzig for some decades to come. Most of the young 'Bremer Beiträger' who signalized themselves by their secession from Gottsched were congregated in the Saxon city. Johann Elias Schlegel, whose comedies breathe the charm and delicacy of Destouches, there wrote *Die stumme Schönheit* (1747), which Lessing describes as 'the best of our original comedies in verse'. Schlegel also made important contribution to dramatic theory, and, in anticipation of Lessing, took up the defence of Shakespeare against Gottsched's attacks. J. A. Ebert became the recognized authority on Young, whose *Night Thoughts* he translated in 1751, and whose influence can be traced in most of the German personal lyrics of the eighteenth century. W. Rabener wrote mild, harmless satires, the subject-matter of which is partly derived from *The Spectator* and other English and German 'moralische Wochenschriften'. J. F. W. Zachariä in his comic epic *Der Renommist* (1744), partly inspired by *The Rape of the Lock*, produced an admirable picture of the student-life of the day.

Chief of all the 'Bremer Beiträger' was C. F. Gellert, like Gottsched a professor at the University of Leipzig ; his reputation as a fabulist has lasted to the present day. To an age in which art was entirely subordinate to morality the fable seemed to be the highest form of poetry. This over-estimation of the fable was due principally to La Fontaine's *Fables* (1668), to the genius of which, however, Gellert could not attain. His *Fabeln und Erzählungen* (1746) are inspired rather by Hagedorn and La Motte, when indeed they are not mere metrical versions of passages collected in the course of his wide reading. But in the homeliness of

their subject-matter, the skilful reproduction of the language
of every-day life, their garrulousness and harmlessness, their
kindly raillery of the weaker sex, and their very obvious and
inevitable moral, they are essentially characteristic of the
German life of the time. Gellert also attained great popularity by his lectures on epistolary style, largely based on
the letters of Madame de Sévigné, which had just appeared
(1726). Goethe, who attended these lectures as a student,
praised them as ' one of the foundations of German culture '.

As a dramatist, Gellert was responsible for the introduction
of the ' comédie larmoyante ' on the model of Nivelle de la
Chaussée and Madame de Graffigny, which he ushered in
with a treatise *Pro Comœdia Commovente* (1751). The
amiable sentimentality of *Die Betschwester*, *Das Loos in der
Lotterie*, *Die zärtlichen Schwestern*, *Die kranke Frau*, made
an immediate appeal to the theatre-going public, and won
from Lessing the praise : ' Of all our comic writers Herr
Gellert is undoubtedly the author whose plays are most
fundamentally German.'

For a professor of moral philosophy the publication of
a remarkable novel, *Die schwedische Gräfin von G**** (1747),
might seem a somewhat risky undertaking. It is a strange
medley of adventures in which the characters become
involved in bigamy and incest, and the action almost belies
the moral intent of the author. But by going to England
for his model Gellert laid the foundation of the modern
German novel. In Richardson's *Pamela*—*Clarissa* appeared
a year too late to be of influence—he found the affecting
sentimentality and the moralizing tendencies he loved, and
adapted them with little regard for Richardson's real merits
as a novelist. In thus introducing Richardson to his fellow-
countrymen Gellert opened up a most fruitful source of
inspiration for German literature ; it has been estimated that

of the 283 German novels written between the years 1774 and 1778 no fewer than one third show the influence of Richardson. Most of them, it is true, were of small literary value, with the possible exception of *Die Geschichte des Fräuleins von Sternheim* (1771) by Sophie von Laroche, which Herder actually rated even higher than *Clarissa*.

When Frau von Laroche asked her kinsman Wieland to write the introduction to her novel, he complied, but with a protest against her perfect Richardsonian characters. For a new influence had in the meanwhile begun to make itself felt in German literature, which Wieland himself was instrumental in introducing. C. M. Wieland (1733–1813) started as a fervent pietist and admirer of Klopstock, but soon swung to the opposite extreme, to the intense grief of his old patron Bodmer. This transformation was effected primarily by his acquaintance with French literature, and Wieland soon found that his real taste lay rather with the loose frivolity of Crébillon, or the brilliant philosophical raillery of Voltaire, than the seraphic poetry of the *Messias*. This conversion which he himself underwent, the victory of the senses over his early moral training, forms the leading motif of nearly all Wieland's works. His heroes, like Agathon for instance, mostly pass through a period of religious 'Schwärmerei' before they attain to the wisdom of an epicurean joy in life, and their love-affairs begin (as in *Oberon*) on a lofty moral plane only to degenerate inevitably into very mundane passions.

It was thus that Wieland (who, incidentally, learnt French from a French translation of *Pamela*) turned from the sententiousness of Richardson's morality to Fielding's realism. His first novel, *Agathon* (not published till 1766), shows him hesitating between the two tendencies : there is still much theorizing about virtue in the Richardsonian vein, but the hero's character is developed and purified through the manifold experiences of life, until he attains the wisdom of the golden mean. Though the scene is laid in ancient Greece, the ideas are essentially modern, and the allusions to Germany are obvious. The chief importance of the novel lies in the attention he has given to the psychological development of his hero ; like Fielding, he is constantly impressing on his readers the fact that he is painting true human character, with all its inconsistencies, not inventing stories. He is thus the founder of the 'Bildungsroman' or 'Entwicklungsroman', that characteristically German product, which passes through *Wilhelm Meister* and *Der junge Tischlermeister* down to *Maler Nolten* and *Der grüne Heinrich* of our own day. In Wieland's next novel, *Don Sylvio von Rosalva* (1764), the triumph of Fielding was complete, as is sufficiently indicated by the sub-title of the book : *Der Sieg der Natur über die Schwärmerei.*

Towards the end of 1767 Wieland made the acquaintance of Laurence Sterne, and was extravagant in his praises. Although his plans for translating *Tristram Shandy* came to nothing, he found himself in such conformity with the Englishman's view of life, with his mingling of wit and sentimentality, that his influence was bound to be very strong. *Der neue Amadis* (1770), and especially *Der goldene Spiegel, oder die Könige von Scheschian* (1772), are patent imitations of Sterne, the former in its erotic tendencies, the latter in style, characterization and humour. This book, which treats of the different forms of government—Wieland's own preference being for the enlightened absolutism of a Frederick II or a Joseph II—was directly responsible for his being called to Weimar as the tutor of the young duke Karl August and his brother. Wieland wrote several other novels with a Greek setting : more valuable was the *Geschichte der Abderiten* (1774), a satiric denunciation under a Greek disguise of the conditions prevalent in German provincial cities.

In his own day Wieland was chiefly renowned for his epic *Oberon* (1780), written in the Italian stanza. It is difficult nowadays to take this fantastic epic seriously. Its theme is a skilful combination of an old French ' chanson de geste' and of Pope's version of *January and May* from Chaucer's *Merchant's Tale*, helped out with some motives from *A Midsummer Night's Dream*. Wieland weaves his fanciful plot with complete indifference to probabilities, he seems to take a malicious delight in the moral failings of his characters, and turns the most tragic situations with a jest. But the epic is nevertheless full of graceful poetry ; its light-hearted delicacy of language was a revelation and a delight to his contemporaries, who, from the high-flown but somewhat heavy strain of Klopstock, had never imagined the German language capable of such lightness and flexibility. The chief merit of Wieland is that he taught Germans the art of narrative that he himself had learned from the English and French; he thereby won a hearing for German literature from French-trained aristocratic circles, which had merely passed by the extravagances of a Klopstock with a smile. In his widely read *Teutscher Merkur* (1773–89), modelled on the famous *Mercure de France*, he kept those same circles in touch with intellectual and political progress in Europe, and was thus instrumental in forming a background of public opinion capable of appreciating the coming revival of German letters.

Wieland also broke new ground by his translation of twenty-two of Shakespeare's plays (1762–6). He was attracted chiefly by the ' marvellous ', by the fairy magic of *The Tempest* and *A Midsummer Night's Dream*, but had little understanding for *Lear* or *Macbeth*, and for some of his renderings of these dramas Herder would have liked ' to scratch out his eyes '. Nevertheless, it was through this partial and one-sided outlook of Wieland that Goethe and Schiller, and the whole of the ' Sturm und Drang ', saw Shakespeare, until Herder presented him under his true aspect.

Wieland had many imitators, especially amongst the laughter-loving Viennese. None of these imitations are of any permanent value, with the exception of the comic epic *Die Jobsiade* (1784) by the Westphalian K. A. Kortum, which, in its time, was as often quoted as Wilhelm Busch in our own day.

III

LESSING

GOTTHOLD EPHRAIM LESSING (1729–81) sums up in his single person all that was great in the eighteenth century. He was the typical ' Aufklärer ', the born fighter ; whether he deals with the drama or the epic, or with religion, he inevitably breaks a lance for truth and reason. ' Had the Almighty given me the choice of either possessing truth or seeking after it, I should have chosen the latter.' This saying of Lessing's characterizes his whole attitude to life, and well describes the man who was to become ' the first critic of Europe '.

Born in the narrow pietistic circles of a Saxon pastor's house, educated under almost monastic conditions at the ' Fürstenschule ' of St. Afra, it was no wonder that when in 1746 he came as a student to Leipzig, the ' Klein Paris ', the centre of rationalistic Germany, he felt very much out of his element. Like Goethe some few years later, he was ashamed of his provincial manners and appearance in this city of elegance and fashion.

Gotthold had been sent to the university with a view to preparing for the traditional family calling of the Lessings, the Lutheran pastorate. But in Leipzig he soon came under the influence of two men who profoundly affected his career : the first, Professor J. F. Christ, the most enlightened and cultured teacher in the university ; the second, Christlob Mylius, Lessing's half-cousin, an avowed free-thinker, who became his best friend and soon instilled into him his own light-hearted philosophy. It was, moreover, through the

influence of Mylius that Lessing, to the horror of the good
folks at home, got into touch with the theatrical company
of Frau Neuber, and thus began that long and intimate
connexion with the theatre which was to end only with his
life.

He entered upon his dramatic apprenticeship with translations from the French ; he tasted the delights of authorship
and induced ' die Neuberin ' to produce a juvenile play,
Der junge Gelehrte ; he gained an accurate and intimate
knowledge of stage-craft which stood him in good stead in
later years. It soon became obvious to him that he was
unfitted for the profession for which he was destined, and
he wrung a reluctant consent from his father to exchange
the theological for the medical faculty. But his university
career came to an abrupt end : he had gone surety for the
Neuber company and, being called upon to make good his
bond, was forced to seek safety in flight. For a time he
hovered in doubt as to whether he should join his former
friends on the stage. Finally wiser counsels prevailed, and
he determined to seek fame and fortune as a journalist in
Berlin.

The harvest of the Leipzig period was not very rich.
Lessing first appeared before the public as a writer of occasional verse some of which was published during the years
1747–8 in the ephemeral periodicals of his friend Mylius,
and collected some years later in a volume entitled *Kleinig-
keiten* (1751). In thus writing anacreontic poetry Lessing
was merely following the fashion of the time, the ' genre '
having been introduced from France into Germany by
Friedrich von Hagedorn. The success of the volume
published by Hagedorn in 1742 gave rise to a host of imitations and notably the *Versuch in scherzhaften Liedern* (1744)
of J. W. L. Gleim. Lessing's ' trifles ' are of a similar type :

love and kisses, wine and song, all purely imaginary. But we shall look in vain for any signs of real lyric feeling such as we occasionally find among the frivolities and unrealities of Goethe's first song-book. Lessing's failure as a lyric poet was perhaps not due so much to inherent defects in himself as to the peculiarity of an age which had not yet been awakened to nature and genuine poetry. There was, more-over, in Lessing's life an almost entire absence of the 'eternal feminine' which is so strongly marked in other poets of the age—in Klopstock, Wieland, Herder, Schiller, not to mention Goethe. It was not until middle age that a woman, Eva König, came into his life, only to die after one short year of wedded happiness.

Lessing showed himself once again as the child of his age in the cultivation of the fable and the epigram. It was not, however, until a later period (1759) that he rediscovered the fable of the ancients. The *Fabeln und Erzählungen* of 1753 are little more than imitations of the licentious *Contes* of La Fontaine or of the Renaissance *Facetiae* of the Italian Poggio. They are devoid of any moral purpose, and all that can be said in their favour is that they are witty and well told. In his *Sinngedichte* (1753), on the other hand, Lessing found a form of literary expression more in accordance with his own genius. He was much addicted to the epigram all his life and, inspired by the great epigrammatist of the seven-teenth century, Friedrich von Logau, wrote valuable *Anmerk-ungen* on the subject (1771). And his best works in this 'genre' belong to this later period.

The most important of Lessing's early works were undoubt-edly his comedies, which showed unmistakable promis of greater things : *Der junge Gelehrte*, performed by Fra Neuber in 1748, is a satire on pedantry ; *Der Freygeis* is a plea for tolerance ; *Die Juden* contains almost th first noble Jew in German literature ; the two latter plays are thus, in a sense, forerunners of *Nathan der Weise*. Three other early plays, *Damon*, *Der Misogyn*, and *Die alte Jungfer*, are essentially juvenile productions, which the author himself later disavowed.

When Lessing arrived in Berlin in 1748 there was not much in the Prussian capital to attract an ambitious young journalist. Frederick the Great, but lately returned home victorious from the war, had, indeed, set up as a patron of literature and art, and had drawn round him at Potsdam a literary circle, of which Voltaire was the chief luminary. But all his interest lay in French literature, and in his eyes no German poem was 'worth a charge of powder'. Nor was Berlin otherwise attractive : it had neither historical tradition nor architectural beauties to appeal to the poet or the artist.

And yet in spite of these drawbacks it was in Berlin that Lessing rose to prominence as critic and author. He served his apprenticeship as a journalist and reviewer on one of its chief papers ; he came into personal contact with Voltaire, and, through the *Lettres anglaises* (1734), first became aware of the existence of English drama. In the preface to the *Beyträge zur Historie und Aufnahme des Theaters* (1750) he mentions Wycherley and Congreve side by side with Shakespeare, but he shows a certain advance on Voltaire's standpoint when he makes the prophetic declaration that 'if German dramatic poetry were to follow its natural impulse it would resemble the English rather than the French form'.

Berlin was to remain the centre of his literary activities for many years. He paid longer or shorter visits to Wittenberg, back to Leipzig, and even started on a European tour as a travelling tutor, but had only reached Holland when he was recalled by the outbreak of the Seven Years War. The years 1760 to 1765 he spent at Breslau as secretary to the governor of the newly conquered province of Silesia. But he always returned to the Prussian capital, which remained his headquarters until 1767. Its great attraction for him was as the centre of the German ' Aufklärung '. A product of the practical English mind of Locke and of the critical sense of Bayle, ' Enlightenment' or Rationalism had been popularized on the Continent by Voltaire. It derived its characteristic German name from the frontispiece of a book of Wolff's, which depicts the dawn breaking through the clouds. In many of its most distinctive features—its practical unimaginative character, its hatred of vague enthusiasms and misty ideals, its determination to apply the test of reason to everything—it necessarily appealed very strongly to Lessing's cold, critical mind, and he was soon on the best of terms with two of the chief exponents of the movement, Mendelssohn and Nicolai.

Moses Mendelssohn (1729–86) was born of poor Jewish parents, and when Lessing first met him was working as a clerk, but had found time outside office hours for extensive reading and high thinking. Here was the noble Jew Lessing had depicted in *Die Juden*. Mendelssohn had the advantage over Lessing of a strict training in philosophy, and from their friendly disputations Lessing gained many a hint for his own critical essays. Under Lessing's auspices Mendelssohn also came forward as an author : without his friend's knowledge Lessing published the *Philosophische Gespräche*. Together they wrote the treatise *Pope ein Metaphysiker !* (1755), in which the chief argument is that the poet and the philosopher must each keep to his own sphere, a foreshadowing in some degree of the *Laokoon*. Mendelssohn's best-known work is the *Phädon* (1767), less a translation from Plato than an attempt to reconcile his belief in the immortality of the soul with the theories of the ' Aufklärung '.

The third in the triumvirate of Berlin ' Aufklärer' was C. F. Nicolai (1733–1811). Like Gottsched, he had the misfortune to outlive his work, but in his youth was in the van of intellectual progress. His *Briefe über den itzigen Zustand der schönen Wissenschaften in Deutschland* (1755) are not on a much lower level than Lessing's critical essays of the time, and his reviews were so good that they were often taken for Lessing's. As the author of the novel *Sebaldus Nothanker* (1773), he has left a most readable and lively account of the society of his own day. But he had not the genius to move with the times, and the tide of progress left him high and dry. In his journal the *Allgemeine Deutsche Bibliothek* (1765–1804) he remained the doughty champion of Rationalism when the latter had long ceased to be a living force. He refused all recognition to the younger generation—he attacked Goethe in his parody *Freuden des jungen Werther* (1775)—and judged everything after his own old-fashioned, prosaic standard. It is no wonder that the younger men retaliated, and showered contempt and abuse upon him : Goethe in the *Walpurgisnacht* and, together with Schiller, in the *Xenien*, the Romanticists with Friedrich Schlegel at their head, the philosophers Kant, Fichte, and Schelling, all had a gibe for Nicolai.

These three friends, Lessing, Mendelssohn, and Nicolai, made Berlin for the moment the chief literary centre in Germany. Their aims and ideals found their best expression in the *Briefe die neueste Literatur betreffend* (1758–65). Lessing himself was the author of only one-sixth of the letters, but the style and method are in any case Lessing's own, which the other contributors imitated so successfully that the authorship of some of the articles is still in question.

The *Literaturbriefe* made a clean sweep of the trammels of pedantry, mediocrity, and arrogance, with which Gottsched

and the Swiss had fettered literature.   It was a much needed
intellectual stimulus to the public, whose taste had been
vitiated by the inanities of the *Moralische Wochenschriften*.
Many of these letters deal severely with the host of bad
translations with which Germany was just then overrun.
One letter bemoans the lack of German historians, another
draws attention to the *Volkslied*, and thus anticipates Herder.
The poet Wieland is adversely criticized for his drama *Lady
Jane Grey* which, according to Lessing, lacked both poetry
and originality ; Cramer's organ, *Der nordische Aufseher*, is
taken to task for its pious narrow-mindedness, whilst the
Messias is declared to be all feeling and very little else.
Bodmer comes in for his share of ridicule, and, as for Gott-
sched, he is satirized out of existence.   The seventeenth
Literaturbrief, which deals with his attempts to reform the
German stage, is a masterpiece of ruthless denunciation.   It
is at the same time a condemnation of the French drama,
and an exhortation to turn rather to Shakespeare and the
English as being far more in harmony with the spirit of the
Greek classics.   And Lessing goes farther : even the old
popular drama which Gottsched had banished from the stage
was more alive, so he avows, was more akin to the German
genius than the tragedy of Corneille.   And in proof of this
he prints the fragment of a play on Faust which ' one of his
friends had sent him '.   If Lessing's *Faust* was ever completed, the manuscript was lost, for the study scene in which
the magician conjures up the fleetest devil of hell to be his
servant is all that has been preserved.   But from the sketch
that remains it appears certain that Lessing's *Faust*, like
Goethe's, was not to succumb to the devil in the end.   In
this championship of the English drama over the French
Lessing had borrowed a hint from Dryden's *Essay of Drama-
tick Poesie*, which he had himself translated in 1758.   From

this time onwards Dryden took a place beside Voltaire as his critical mentor, until he finally led him to the definitely anti-French standpoint of the *Hamburgische Dramaturgie*.

Lessing was not alone in his struggle against tradition in literature : he found an unexpected ally in his French contemporary Denis Diderot, 'than whom, since Aristotle, no more philosophic spirit has busied himself with the theatre '. The latter, too, had cast about for a drama that should be in conformity with the spirit of the age, and he had found it in the ' comédie larmoyante '. While tragedy proper still remained the preserve of the nobility, the new enlightened French ' bourgeoisie ' had raised comedy to unexampled heights of pathos and sentiment. In *Le Fils naturel* (1757) and *Le Père de famille* (1758), Diderot gives full scope to both tendencies, and Lessing was moved to translate the plays almost immediately in his *Theater des Herrn Diderot* (1760).

The ' comédie larmoyante' was mainly of French origin; the ' bürgerliches Trauerspiel ', or tragedy of common life, on the other hand, came from England, where the middle classes had risen to even greater political and social importance. Lessing had expressed this view in the *Theatralische Bibliothek* (1754-8) for which he translated Gellert's treatise *Das rührende Lustspiel*. He proposed similarly to discuss the ' bürgerliches Trauerspiel ', when he found that Diderot had anticipated him. Instead of the theory, he gave the world a practical illustration in *Miss Sara Sampson* (1755).

In his *Merchant of London* (1731) George Lillo had broken new ground by presenting upon the stage an incident of everyday life played by everyday people. It is the sordid story of an apprentice, who, in spite of the love of his master's daughter, is seduced by the wiles of a harlot to murder his uncle for the sake of his gold. After a tearful prison-scene between the lovers, the play ends with preparations for the execution of the murderer and his mistress upon the stage. There is a certain correspondence of characters between this drama and *Miss Sara Sampson*, but there the similarity ends ; Lessing's drama bears but little resemblance to the crude melodrama with its purely didactic purpose. For his plot he had recourse to Richardson's *Clarissa Harlowe*. Here, too, we have the pure-minded girl who has eloped with an amiable libertine and is eating out her heart in repentance at a village inn. It is not only in the motifs and in the borrowing of a few names that Lessing shows his dependence on Richardson, it is rather in the whole atmosphere and especially in the heightened moral sensibility. He had not yet learned, however, to combine these numerous motifs harmoniously together— the intrigue is not free from improbabilities, the dialogue is wearisome in its diffuseness. Nor has he entirely emancipated himself from the shackles of French tradition : he has, it is true, chosen his characters from the middle classes (though still from the upper middle classes), but he observes two of the unities strictly, and the unity of place he transgresses only once. In the servants we have the inevitable confidants of the ' haute tragédie ', and the classical influence is still strong enough to make Marwood poison herself off the stage.

It is difficult nowadays to share the enthusiasm with which the German public received *Miss Sara Sampson* for more than a generation. To us the play is mainly of interest as the first ' bürgerliches Trauerspiel ' on the English model, and its success may best be gauged by the numerous imitations it called forth : Lessing's own *Emilia Galotti* and Goethe's *Clavigo* and *Stella* are its direct descendants. But the more notable exponents of the ' bürgerliches Trauerspiel ' are F. L. Schröder (1744–1816), the prolific A. W.

Iffland (1759–1814), and A. Kotzebue (1761–1819), of whom the latter, with his 214 dramas, was the most popular playwright in Europe for a whole generation. The ' drama of common life ' held the German stage until well on in the nineteenth century, with the plays of Charlotte Birch-Pfeiffer, Bauernfeld, Benedix, and Gutzkow, and the list includes Hebbel's *Maria Magdalena*, in which the middle-class sentiments which found such favour with Lessing's contemporaries are represented in their narrowness and pettiness as the bane of modern life.

Lessing's next and greatest play, *Minna von Barnhelm* (1767), was the first German drama to be penetrated with a vigorous national feeling, the first to describe German characters and manners with realistic truth. It was as such that it struck Goethe, who, in his famous criticism in *Dichtung und Wahrheit*, VIII, describes it as ' the most genuine production of the Seven Years War . . . the first dramatic work which drew its subject from the greater public life and from contemporary events '. The setting is entirely modern : the action takes place at a Berlin hostelry on August 22, 1763, but a few months after peace had been signed. It presents a realistic picture of the contrasts, the rancour and the general unrest which follow everywhere in the wake of a great war. It is an attempt in the sphere of literature to reconcile Prussian and Saxon by representing the French as the real enemy. Not that Lessing avowed any such intention ; like Goethe he was far too much of a ' Weltbürger ' to be a patriot, and had as little use for such ' heroic weakness '. Although the great figure of Frederick looms as the ' deus ex machina ' in the background, the play is no apology for Prussian militarism. Lessing's ideal soldier von Tellheim is significantly not a Prussian by birth, and, far from considering soldiering as the only possible career for a gentleman, longs rather for the time when he will be able to doff his uniform and retire to his estates. Tellheim owes much to Lessing's friend Kleist : he has the same noble manliness tinged with melancholy ; something of Lessing's own personality has passed over into his hero. For the first time in German comedy we have the serious elderly lover, a man as free from trifling as from the desire to make a rich marriage. Minna herself is in many respects the counterpart of Lessing : he has endowed her with all his gaiety, his warm heart, and above all with his clear-sighted intellect which she uses with an obstinacy that is decidedly masculine. It is apparent that there is not much room for comedy in the clash of two such serious personalities and, indeed, at times the action threatens to take an almost tragic turn. To relieve the tension, and also to justify the title to comedy, Lessing has introduced the typical comic figures of the followers, Werner and Franziska. But he has idealized the traditional servants of comedy into two of the most original characters of the play. Amongst the minor characters, Just and the widow of Tellheim's brother-officer provide the sentimental element, which was the delight of contemporary audiences. The chief relic of the older comedy is to be found in Riccaut de la Marlinière, the bragging, swaggering, unscrupulous adventurer of tradition. In investing him with French nationality, Lessing provides a foil to the German Tellheim, and his broken German furnishes the traditional farcical interlude.

From his vast store of literary reading Lessing drew many details for *Minna von Barnhelm* : he owes something to Regnard's *Le Joueur*, more to Farquhar's *Constant Couple* and *The Beaux' Stratagem*, and there are also reminiscences of Destouches and Diderot. The latter's ' drame sérieux ' with its deep feeling and moralizing tone was one of the chief

models Lessing had before him. But if the plot is not very
original, the style, at least, is entirely Lessing's own. This
comedy of Lessing established a new language of the stage :
the dialogue is brilliant and the characters are admirably por-
trayed by their conversation. The technique of the play is
as perfect as its style. Much of its dramatic effect is obtained
by the strict application of the unities ; the first two acts
Goethe declared to be 'a masterpiece of exposition', and as
an old man he could still recall the extraordinary enthusiasm
with which the play was received by the younger generation.
Minna von Barnhelm still ranks (with a reservation perhaps
in favour of Grillparzer's *Weh dem, der lügt*) as the greatest
comedy of German literature.

From the point of view of literary history *Minna von
Barnhelm* was the forerunner of numerous ' Soldatenstücke '
of which no less than 260 appeared within fifty years. None
of them rise above mediocrity, and it remained for a later
kinsman of Tellheim's model, Heinrich von Kleist, to re-
juvenate the subject by endowing it with a new and deeper
psychology in his *Prinz Friedrich von Homburg*.

The second great production of the Breslau period was
the *Laokoon, oder über die Grenzen der Mahlerey und Poesie*
(1766). Lessing's interest in aesthetics was first aroused
by Mendelssohn, who, as early as 1756, had pointed out to
him the importance of a new book by J. J. Winckelmann
(1717–68) on Greek sculpture. To Goethe and his contemporaries Winckelmann was 'a literary Columbus' who
had rediscovered Greek art. He proclaimed its ideals, its
' noble simplicity and calm greatness ' as a gospel and revealed
to the eighteenth century ' its great and grave soul ' : ' As
the depths of the sea always remain calm, however much the
surface may be raging, so the expression in the figures of the
Greeks, under every form of passion, shows a great and self-

collected soul '. In this book Winckelmann went on to
compare the late Greek Laocoon group with Virgil's description and finds that the expression of pain is different in each
case : the poet expresses pain most realistically and awakens
our pity ; the sculptor shows us pain subdued by human
strength of character and awakens both pity and admiration.
Which was the greater of the two, the poet or the painter ?

Lessing welcomed Mendelssohn's reference to Winckelmann, less because he was interested in Greek art than
because it furnished him with the long-sought weapon of
offence against descriptive poetry. He had already had many
a tilt at the riot of description in modern poetry ; his ideas
on the subject had been gradually taking shape, until they
were crystallized in the *Laokoon*.

Laocoon, as represented in the celebrated statue in the
Vatican, does not open his mouth wide enough to utter a
shriek, such as he utters in Virgil. As it can be shown that
the cry of bodily pain is perfectly compatible with Greek
notions of bravery, why did the artist differ from the poet
in the representation of the pain of Laocoon ? It is, says
Lessing, because of the fundamental difference between
plastic art and poetry, and the different materials in which
they work. While painting, for instance, represents co-
existing objects in space, poetry expresses consecutive objects
in time ; the one deals with bodies, the other with actions.
The poet should avoid description, for, by the time he has
finished the enumeration of the various traits, we shall already
have forgotten the first, and gain no clear notion of the whole.
Painting is much more apt for description. Instead of
describing beauty, the poet will attain his object much more
effectively if he describes the effect the beautiful object
produces on others ; he must transmute beauty in a state of
repose into beauty in action, in other words into grace.

But whilst poetry should not describe beauty in repose, so too painting should avoid depicting the ugly or the disgusting, for it would soon become repulsive from its very fidelity to nature. As with beauty, so with ugliness : by a successive enumeration of its various elements, the force of the effect will be much diminished. It is possible then for poetry to depict ugliness without causing too much disgust. Since the artist must concentrate his picture in a single moment, he must take great care to choose the right moment, that ' pregnant moment ' which allows the freest scope to the imagination. It must therefore not be the extreme point of the passion represented, else the imagination could not soar beyond.

The aim of this little book is then quite clear : it is directed primarily against the mania for description, in which German poetry of the eighteenth century, of Brockes, Zachariä, Klopstock, Haller, Kleist, Gessner, abounds ; but by insisting that the essence of poetry was action it helped unintentionally to prepare the way for the 'Sturm und Drang'.

In his *Dichtung und Wahrheit* Goethe has described the effect which the *Laokoon* had on the rising generation : ' The so long misunderstood " Ut pictura poesis " was at once abolished. . . . Like lightning all the consequences of that splendid thought flashed upon us ; all former criticism was flung away like a worn-out garment.' But the influence of the *Laokoon* on German literature was subconscious rather than direct ; Goethe, for instance, translates the charms of Lotte or Dorothea into motion, while his lyric poetry is strangely free from all descriptions of female beauty. It is not, however, in having curtailed the tendency to descriptive poetry that the chief merit of the *Laokoon* lies, nor in its delimitation of the sphere of poetry and painting. Lessing's work in this respect was undone by men like Tieck and Wackenroder, and in our own day the cinematograph has succeeded in confusing the whole issue. The importance of the treatise lies rather in its critical reasoning, the careful and logical composition, the facility of its language and the sharpness of its wit.

The book is valuable also for the insight it affords into the nature of poetry. On this matter, we feel, Lessing speaks with authority. When he writes on art, on the other hand, it is apparent that he was but poorly equipped for the position of ' Kunstrichter ' to which he aspired. The best works of the best Greek period were still unknown at the time, and Lessing's knowledge was derived either from pictures of Roman imitations or from text-books. Lessing, moreover, looked upon art purely from the intellectual, un-emotional, theoretical standpoint of the typical ' Aufklärer '.

In the appreciation of Lessing's great treatise the fact must not be overlooked that others had prepared the way for him, and that the *Laokoon* was but the culmination of a movement which had been in progress for some time. Lessing owed something to J. B. Dubos and Breitinger and to the English critics J. Harris and Spence, more to Diderot's *Lettres sur les Sourds et les Muets* (1751). But, if most of these critics were clear concerning the essential differences of painting and poetry, Lessing was the first to point out the abuses which resulted from the neglect of these differences.

Lessing had completed the book somewhat hastily— ' These are rather jottings for a book than an actual book ' he had written of it—because for a moment there seemed a delightful prospect of his obtaining the Royal Librarianship at Berlin, and the *Laokoon* was to prove his scholarly fitness for such a post. But Frederick's prejudice against German men of letters in general, and his private animosity towards Lessing in particular—Voltaire while still a guest of the

Prussian king had calumniated his German confrère—spoiled his chances from the first, and the post was bestowed upon some unworthy Frenchman. This undeserved slight so disgusted Lessing with Berlin that he accepted with alacrity a tempting offer to act as dramatic adviser for a new theatrical venture at Hamburg.

Hamburg, where Lessing arrived in 1767, had behind it a long reputation for drama and opera, and its wealth and prosperity made it a happy hunting-ground for all the strolling players of the time. The National Theatre, however, like so many undertakings of the kind, was doomed to failure for lack of funds, and was forced to close its doors within little more than a year. Ephemeral as was the enterprise, Lessing has rendered its name immortal. Twice a week a journal was published containing criticisms of plays and actors : these are the famous papers known as the *Hamburgische Dramaturgie*.

The *Dramaturgie* may be divided into two parts, a negative and a positive. To the first belongs the critical discussion of the pieces played ; the positive side culminates in the discussion of Aristotle's definition of tragedy. While the first part affords a valuable insight into the repertory of contemporary Germany—it is characteristic of the conditions of the German stage that the proportion of comedy to tragedy was approximately five to one—it is obvious that the critical discussion of a play entails previous acquaintance with that play, or it is incomprehensible. But scattered amongst these criticisms are valuable observations relating to such general questions as the abuse of the heroic in tragedy, the introduction of the supernatural, the treatment of historical sources, the construction of a plot, and, above all, the unity of character. This latter consideration leads to the essence of the treatise, the investigation of Aristotle's definition of tragedy.

' Tragedy ', such is the gist of Aristotle's definition, ' by arousing pity and fear effects the purification (Katharsis) of such emotions.' The conception of the theory which Lessing combated was that enunciated by Corneille : that the aim of tragedy was, through the representation of pity *or* terror, to put the spectator on his guard against the extravagance of passion and to teach him the necessity of moderation and self-control.

Lessing first concerned himself with the question during the years 1756–8, when he discussed Aristotle's theory in his letters to Nicolai and Mendelssohn. His positive contribution to the discussion at this time was his insistence that the correct translation of the Greek ' phobos ' was ' fear ' and not ' terror ', although he was by no means the first critic to make this distinction. But he is far removed from the true interpretation of Aristotle when he concludes that the main object of tragedy is to increase the consciousness of our personality, which is involved in every great emotion. What arouses pity for others will arouse fear for ourselves and so teach us the virtue of sympathy. Tragic pleasure, then, is sympathy.

Lessing did not return seriously to the study of Aristotle until 1768, at a time when the *Dramaturgie* was nearing its end. In the meanwhile he had modified somewhat his interpretation of the difficult passage : Tragedy is said to purify pity and fear because the frequent excitement of these emotions in the theatre has a tendency to weaken their force, and so moderate and reduce them to a just measure, and thus : ' The tragic purification of the passions consists merely in the conversion of pity and fear into virtuous habits of mind.' It is clear that Lessing paraphrases rather than explains Aristotle ; the error lies in the moral meaning which Lessing and other contemporary critics insisted on reading into the term ' Katharsis ' which, according to the modern Greek scholar, is nothing more nor less than a term borrowed from medicine, a view with which the eighteenth century itself was not unfamiliar. As an occasional purge was considered requisite to expel the peccant humours from the body, so tragic excitement will lighten the soul of man from its accumulated emotion, and afford him the pleasure of relief.

One feels, however, that Lessing was really concerned not so much to interpret Aristotle correctly as to confute the dramatic theory and practice of the French, especially of Corneille, and, by implication, of Voltaire. Having proved satisfactorily that Corneille's reading of Aristotle was wrong when he maintained that tragedy might excite pity or fear, not necessarily both in the same drama, it was easy enough to show that his dramas, judged by the Aristotelian theory, must be rejected, and with them the whole classic drama, since, the foundation having been destroyed, the whole edifice necessarily tumbled to the ground. The French authors, Lessing concludes, ' could not be other than clever men ; some of them deserve no mean rank among the poets . . . but they have little or nothing of that which makes Sophocles, Euripides and Shakespeare what they are'.

In thus opposing the Greek and English drama to the French, Lessing tacitly assumes that Shakespeare unconsciously followed the ideal of Sophocles, while the truth is that, if Corneille must fall by the Aristotelian doctrines, so must Shakespeare : for example, *Richard III* excites fear, even terror, but scarcely pity. If Polyeucte is condemned because he has done nothing to deserve his fate, then Cordelia must be rejected as well. In spite of the occasional references in the *Dramaturgie* to *Richard III* and other plays of Shakespeare Lessing never faces the issue honestly ; he was content to find in the English dramatist a model of dramatic art whom he could oppose successfully to the Classical school of the

French and he did not concern himself with the revolutionary effect of his discovery. By his rejection of the conventions of the French theatre, he had unintentionally weakened all authority based on dramatic rules, and so opened up the way for the unbridled licence of the ' Sturm und Drang '.

That Lessing was not in earnest when he pointed to Shakespeare as the model for the German stage to imitate is proved by the fact that he himself did not follow his own precepts. His next drama, *Emilia Galotti* (1772), is essentially a tragedy of conflict after the French model : it is a perfect example of a concise, dramatic action, leading by a series of carefully gradated scenes to the inevitable catastrophe. It even retains most of the Classical externals : the principle of ' ideale Ferne ', the rhetorical character of the language, even to the notorious unities. The unity of time is observed completely ; change of scene takes place only twice.

Lessing emphasized the fact that his *Emilia Galotti* was no more than the old Roman story of Virginia in a new garb ; but whereas in ancient Rome a father had power of life and death over his children, such an action was obviously impossible under modern conditions, and it is difficult to find adequate motives for Odoardo's deed. It is only by a direct appeal to his reason, by using language and arguments entirely out of keeping with her character and upbringing, that Emilia can induce her father to deal the fatal blow. It was doubtless the artificiality of the denouement that drew from Goethe the adverse criticism that *Emilia Galotti* was ' only imagined '. On the other hand, there is nothing more modern in German literature than Emilia's struggle between love and honour. She dies because she fears to yield willingly to the prince ; it is a subtle conception of a woman's individuality, which foreshadows the psychological conflicts of Hebbel's heroines.

Undoubtedly the most dramatic figure of the play is the Countess Orsina, the forsaken mistress of the prince, the most passionate of all Lessing's women. From the literary point of view she is the counterpart of Marwood in *Miss Sara Sampson*, but is definitely her superior in characterization. In the scene in which she urges Odoardo to avenge her honour and his own on the man who has betrayed them both, Orsina reaches a height of tragic irony which was certainly not attained by her counterpart Lady Milford in *Kabale und Liebe*. As a literary model, indeed, *Emilia Galotti* is of supreme importance : Marinelli is, according to a witty remark of Börne, ' the grandfather of all stage court-villains ', and most of the characters reappear in one guise or another in the German drama of the next generation.

Lessing had finally found a resting-place from his wanderings as librarian to the Duke of Brunswick in Wolfenbüttel, which was to remain his home for the rest of his life. His last years were embittered by the virulent controversy which he waged with his friend of earlier days, Pastor Goeze of Hamburg, concerning the credibility of Biblical miracles, Lessing, of course, adopting the purely negative attitude of rationalism. The fight was waged with varying fortune. Finally Goeze most unfairly appealed to the higher ecclesiastical authorities, and the Duke of Brunswick deprived Lessing of his freedom from the censorship. Balked in one direction, Lessing reverted to his old pulpit, the stage. If he were not permitted to expound his views concerning natural religion in polemical pamphlets, he would do so through the mouth of his sage Jew. Deliberately he chose as the centre-piece of his drama Boccaccio's well-known parable of the rings, and built his fable around it. This necessarily entailed some artificiality of construction,

which is further heightened by the improbabilities of the
plot.   It has been shown that Lessing had originally in view
a ' tragédie bourgeoise ' of the type of Diderot—Nathan
himself would make an admirable ' père de famille '—but,
as his needs for a platform grew, changed his plans and wrote
a problem play.   In this he was influenced by the example
of Voltaire, and indebted especially to the latter's *Les Guèbres
ou la Tolérance* and *Zaïre*, with both of which *Nathan* has
many points in common.   From Voltaire, too, he derived
the pseudo-oriental setting.   Indeed, no drama of Lessing's
is more akin to the French ideal than *Nathan der Weise* ;
none of his characters approach more nearly to dramatic
types than Nathan or Saladin.   Lessing was not concerned
with the development of his characters—there is virtually
none in the play—but only to present his religious ideas in
the most telling form.   And whatever criticism may be
levelled against *Nathan der Weise* as a drama, as a philosophical poem of ideas it stands in the first rank : ' He who
understands *Nathan* knows Lessing ', said Friedrich Schlegel,
and, indeed, in its championship of humanity against obscur-
antism, of universal brotherhood against nationalism, of
cosmopolitan philanthropy against narrow sectarianism, it is
a magnificent monument, not only to Lessing, but to German
humanitarianism and enlightenment in the eighteenth century.

In one sense *Nathan der Weise* may also be said to have
opened up a new era for the German drama : it was the
first important play to be written in blank verse, which,
through Lessing's authority, was thus to be raised to the
accepted medium of the higher German drama.   *Nathan der
Weise* appeared early in 1779—it was the last great poetic
work Lessing was destined to undertake.   The remaining
two years of his life—he died February 15, 1781—were

devoted to a defence of freemasonry entitled *Ernst und Falk*, and to the completion of his *Erziehung des Menschengeschlechts* (1780). In these aphorisms is expressed the same great ideal of humanitarianism as in *Nathan der Weise*; it was, as it were, Lessing's final and lasting testament to mankind. He looks forward to 'that time of a new eternal gospel that shall come on earth', when men will 'do good for the sake of the good', without hope of other reward beyond the enrichment of their own spiritual life.

IV

HERDER AND THE
GÖTTINGER BUND

WHILE Lessing may be considered as the culmination
of the German eighteenth century, Herder ushers in our
modern world. Through his influence the protracted controversy between the Ancients and Moderns was decided
definitely in favour of the latter, and, as the founder of the
literary movement of the 'Sturm und Drang', Herder
became one of the greatest forces in German literature for
the next fifty years.

Herder was a thinker, a critic, an historian, a philosopher,
a preacher and orator, rather than a man of letters. He
began many books indeed, and finished none ; but it was
less the form than the ideas with which his fragments are
impregnated that mattered.

Until well on in the sixties of the eighteenth century, in
spite of the *Messias* and pietism, rationalism still held sway
in German intellectual life. Since Opitz introduced the
canons of the Renaissance, German literature had been limited
to the conscious imitation of the Ancients. But we have
seen how under the influence of the English, of Young,
Richardson, and Sterne, one German poet after another
grew restive in the yoke of artificiality. The decisive
impulse undoubtedly came from J. J. Rousseau (1712–78).
Through him the Germans learned with astonishment that
reason was no reliable guide for man's conduct, that, on the
other hand, the divine voice of his heart and his conscience
alone was infallible, and capable of bringing him happiness.

Rousseau taught (without any show of historical justification indeed) that mankind, before baneful knowledge came to them, lived in a care-free state of perfect happiness, and that civilization had been the ruin of that golden age. Hence all Rousseau's writings turn on that one thought : ' back to nature ! ' In his attacks on the privileges of the nobility, his plea for the natural rights of man, and his theory of the state as a voluntary social contract, Rousseau was the immediate forerunner of the French Revolution.

It was less his political ideas that appealed to the Germans than his views on social reform. The theme of his *Nouvelle Héloïse* (1760), especially that of the love of the poor tutor for the lady of high degree, was the subject of innumerable variations by the ' Stürmer und Dränger '. Rousseau would allow full bent to the feelings in this as in all other problems of life : and that naturalness, the loss of which he deplored in society, he affected to find in the unspoiled children of the soil, in peasants, in savages, and especially in children. In literature the application of his theories meant the negation of all criticism ; not culture, and above all not theoretical canons of taste, whether derived from the French or the Greeks, made the poet, but the inspiration of a full heart seeking expression, and that alone : ' Gefühl ist alles,' says Goethe in *Faust*, and ' Wenn ihr's nicht fühlt, ihr werdet's nie erjagen.' Originality and nationality were the catchwords bandied on all sides ; truth to nature led to the crudest realism, ugliness and squalor are deemed as worthy of representation as beauty and splendour ; with the realism of the theme went hand in hand the realism of form ; prose was preferred to verse as being more natural ; and the poet's passionate temperament found expression in the incoherence and exclamatory nature of his utterances.

The first German to give expression to these theories was

Herder's fellow-countryman J. G. Hamann, whose obscure and oracular utterances gained for him the title ' Der Magus im Norden '. From him Herder learnt the meaning of individuality, of enthusiasm, of a whole-hearted love of nature. Hamann took up and developed from the *Conjectures on Original Composition* Young's doctrine of the poet as the heaven-inspired genius, who is born and not made, and he pointed out to his pupil the greatness of primitive poetry, of the Bible, Homer, Shakespeare. Poetry, he maintained in a phrase which Herder was to borrow from him, was the ' mother-tongue of the human race '. Most of these ideas of Hamann, stripped indeed of their mystic garb, we shall find again in Herder. From Hamann, too, Herder learnt English, using *Hamlet* as a text-book.

Herder remained for two years at Königsberg ' studying, teaching, and dreaming '. It was on Hamann's recommendation that he obtained a post as schoolmaster in Riga, which he soon exchanged for an important cure of souls at two of the city churches. The first-fruits of these years of preparation were the *Fragmente über die neuere deutsche Literatur* (1767), written with the express purpose of continuing the *Literaturbriefe* of Lessing, which had ceased to appear in 1765. Nor was Herder's critical standpoint as yet very different from that of Lessing ; the chief distinction was one of method. Whereas the *Literaturbriefe* are casual reviews, devoid of any interconnexion, Herder succeeded in providing a coherent picture of German literature. We find here for the first time the conception of literature as the reflection of a definite, national civilization, to be judged not from any preconceived standard, but entirely in the light of historical development. It is the critic's duty, then, not to judge books, but the spirit which animates them, to discover the creative principles underlying them, of which they are merely the outward expression.

And not only must each literature be submitted to this
scrutiny, but each individual author, and even each of his
separate works. Herder thus became the founder of the
scientific study of literature. Obviously the source and
medium of all intellectual activity is language, which, for
Herder, was a living organism, an organic growth. This
discovery of Herder's was the starting-point of the modern
science of philology.

While the *Fragmente* were in the nature of a continuation of the *Literaturbriefe*, Herder's next work, *Kritische
Wälder* (so called in imitation of Quintilian's *Silvae*),
already betrayed a certain antagonism to the classicism of
Lessing. Although at one with the author of the *Laokoon*
in condemning descriptive poetry, he yet took exception
to Lessing's definition of poetry—arbitrary signs successive
in time, he maintains, would characterize music, the dance,
even ordinary speech equally well. He sees rather the
essence of poetry in ' energy ', a word pregnant with meaning
for the coming ' Kraftgenies ' of the ' Sturm und Drang '.
This energy he finds especially in Homer, who compares
favourably with Virgil in this respect.

Meanwhile the pettiness of his surroundings in Riga
began to oppress Herder, and in the summer of 1769 he
preached his farewell sermon to his sorrowing flock and took
ship for Nantes, from there to pass on to Paris. He has put
on record the profound impression which this journey made
upon him in his *Journal meiner Reise im Jahre 1769*. Herder
is one of the few German poets who have felt themselves
attracted by the sea, as the Greeks and English are attracted
by it. It not only suggested to him a new aspect of the
poetry of the Greeks as a seafaring people, but he was filled
with the desire to know more of the countries past which he
sailed, to study their history and their present conditions,

and to apply the results of his investigations to the reform of Russia, his adopted country. The misty shores of England call up visions of Fingal and Ossian. The brain of this young man of twenty-four teemed with magnificent fancies : he planned a work on German literature and philosophy, a history of human and Christian culture, a new translation of the Bible and a Life of Christ. Most of the projects were never fulfilled ; many of them became merged in the *Ideen zur Philosophie der Geschichte der Menschheit.*

Herder, though he made the acquaintance of Diderot and d'Alembert, was rather repelled than attracted by the intellectual atmosphere of the French capital ; its external magnificence awakened the consciousness of his German nationality, and he was glad to accept the tempting offer of a travelling tutorship to the heir-apparent of a petty German sovereign. On his way home he seized the opportunity of making the acquaintance of Lessing, still lingering in Hamburg after the failure of his theatrical venture. Here, too, he found a kindred spirit in the homely Holstein poet, Matthias Claudius.

This ' grand tour ' was a disappointment in many respects, although it is true that a sojourn in Darmstadt brought him the acquaintance of his future wife, Caroline Flachsland. But the slights he received from the aristocratic entourage induced him to part company with the prince ; moreover he was troubled with an eye affection which rendered medical attention imperative. For six months he remained in Strasbourg, undergoing several operations, and often confined to a dark room. It was during this period that Goethe, then a young student at the university, paid him a formal visit which was the prelude of a warm friendship. In his autobiography Goethe unreservedly acknowledges his debt to Herder. Above all Herder expounded to him the importance of Young's famous *Conjectures on Original Composition*, the knowledge of which he himself owed to Hamann. ' Genius ', says Young, ' can set us right in composition, without the rules of the learned,' and again : ' The less we copy the renowned ancients, the more we shall resemble them.' It was thus that Herder taught Goethe to regard poetry ' in another sense ', and in illustration of these theories sent him to the study of primitive poetry. Thus it was that Goethe, through Herder, became the leader of that revolt against con- vention which is known in German literature as the ' Sturm und Drang '.

The immediate literary expression of this communion between the two poets was a publication *Von deutscher Art und Kunst*, which did not actually appear, however, until 1773. Of the five essays it contains, two are by Herder, another by Goethe. The *Briefwechsel über Ossian* shows Herder, like most of his contemporaries in France and England, com- pletely under the spell of the impostor Macpherson. Here, he thought, was the ' original ' poet whom Young had fore- told ; here was the inspired poetry of a primitive people, real folk-poetry which reflected the actual living world around, and the directness of which could only be matched by the greatest poets, such as Homer or Shakespeare. From this we pass to Herder's second essay on Shakespeare. No pro- founder appreciation of the very essence of Shakespeare's poetical nature, set against the background of his age, has ever been written, and it is Herder's finest piece of literary criticism. Again, however, he owes much to Hamann's conception of the poet as the ' vessel of the creative deity '. Shakespeare is the Heaven-inspired genius whose work is regulated not by laws derived from men, even if those be demi-gods like the Greeks, but is created out of the fulness of the poet's own being. Herder conceives of God, much as Goethe did later, as the creator and inspirer of all things, as pantheistically present throughout the universe, which is itself but the manifestation of the deity, ' der Gottheit lebendiges Kleid '. For Herder, Shakespeare is part and parcel of nature, his works but one of her numerous manifestations ; they are true and great, because they are the expression of life in all its manifold activities, because they are life itself. Herder's approach to Shakespeare was thus diametrically opposed to that of Lessing : while Lessing subjected him to criticism, tested him by the touchstone of the Greek drama, and found him not wanting, Herder identified his art with the creative process itself and saw the function of criticism in identifying itself with that process. In other words, Herder opposed feeling to reason and sought the method of approach through the poet himself rather than through the critic.

If Herder had found it easy to resign his tutorship, it was because better and more congenial prospects were opened up to him by the offer of the chief pastorate of the small state of Schaumburg-Lippe. Although the post did not realize all his expectations, it at least rendered possible his marriage, for which occasion Goethe wrote a satire on his friend, *Ein Fastnachtspiel vom Pater Brey*, showing little discretion or taste, which marked the beginning of the gradual estrangement of the two poets. Herder spent five and a half years in Bückeburg, years of considerable literary activity. Apart from the two essays already mentioned, and the numerous articles contributed to his new review, the *Frankfurter Gelehrte Anzeigen*, and to Nicolai's *Allgemeine deutsche Bibliothek*, the chief work of this period was a small book of 190 pages, which appeared in 1775 under the odd title, *Auch eine Philosophie der Geschichte zur Bildung der Menschheit*. It contains incidentally an enthusiastic defence of the Middle Ages, which are contrasted, as the ages of faith and feeling, with the cold reason of rationalism and, like Goethe's warm championship of Gothic architecture published two years earlier, is significant of the new attitude towards the German past, which Romanticism was to bring into prominence a few years later. The remaining works of the Bückeburg period deal mainly with matters of exegesis, and are more of the nature of theological treatises than pure literature. *Die älteste Urkunde des Menschengeschlechts* (1774), in spite of the extravagance of style and conception, does however consider the Bible as the national literature of the Jews, and seeks to explain it from this point of view, an attempt to which Herder returned later in *Vom Geiste der ebräischen Poesie* (1782–3). The most interesting of these lesser publications is the prize essay *Ursachen des gesunknen Geschmacks bei den verschiednen Völkern* (1775), in which, true to his principles, he ascribes to French influence the low level of taste in Europe at that time.

In the meanwhile Herder had in 1776 at Goethe's instance exchanged the drowsiness of Bückeburg for the more exhilarating atmosphere of Weimar, which, in spite of several attempts to lure him elsewhere, remained his home until his death in 1803. The years spent in Weimar were not entirely happy : Herder's hasty and satiric temper, very prompt to take offence, his constant financial difficulties, his want of sympathy with the free-thinking court circles, the gradual estrangement from Goethe, who had completely usurped the literary position to which he thought himself entitled, the petty quarrel with his old master Kant, were so many disadvantages and vexations for which his friendship with the poet Wieland and the Duchess Luise offered only moderate compensation. Moreover his position as chief pastor was no sinecure, and left him with little leisure to indulge his favourite literary occupations. The output of his last years is consequently rather of the nature of summary or recapitulation. Of the greatest importance was the fruition of his life-long interest in the *Volkslied*. Begun in the Strasbourg period with the active co-operation of Goethe, his collection of folk-songs had grown sufficiently to enable him to publish two parts of *Volkslieder* (1778–9), to which a later editor gave the famous title of *Stimmen der Völker in Liedern.* Although largely inspired by Bishop Percy's *Reliques of Ancient Poetry* (1765), Herder's conception of the *Volkslied* was much more catholic than that of his model ; all 'primitive' poetry was equally welcome, and Herder's definition was wide enough to include Sappho, Pindar, Ossian, Shakespeare (the extracts were based on Dodd's *Beauties of Shakespeare*), as well as *Chevy Chase*, and songs from Kamtschatka and far Peru. Herder was particularly successful in reproducing the form and feeling of the originals. For the first time in history poetry is here represented as the universal language of mankind ; and the collection prepared the way for that new conception of ' world literature ' which Goethe, and especially the Romanticists, did much to propagate, while at the same time it laid the foundations of the modern study of comparative literature. By insisting on the need for sincerity and feeling, it put an end once for all to the conventional poetry of the day.

Herder pursued the same train of thought in *Der Cid. Nach Spanischen Romanzen besungen* (not published until 1805, after the author's death). The title is somewhat misleading : it is less a translation from the Spanish than an adaptation of the French text from the *Bibliothèque universelle des romans.* It is nevertheless the most artistically finished of his writings, and he shows here to perfection his rare capacity for assimilating and reproducing the poetry of another nation so as to make it entirely his own.

The main achievement of Herder's last years is his *Ideen zur Philosophie der Geschichte der Menschheit* (1784–91) in which all his former theories are condensed. The history of mankind is here considered under the aspect of the natural development of human forces and impulses in relation to time and space. The ideal is perfect humanity to be attained by true culture, to which poetry, art, science, and above all religion, are the chief means of approach. The greatest triumph of ideal humanism Herder now discovered in the Greeks or in the Renaissance, rather than in the Middle Ages. The *Ideen* was one of Goethe's favourite books, and, to a large extent, formed the theoretical basis on which the whole edifice of the classical achievement was built. Later philosophers, Schelling, Hegel, Lotze, are deep in its debt. To the modern reader the *Ideen* seem largely commonplaces ; they have been so thoroughly assimilated in our culture that it is difficult to realize the enormous impression they made on the author's contemporaries.

One of Herder's last important works, *Briefe zu Beförderung der Humanität* (1793–7), defines his political creed. Almost alone amongst the great German poets Herder was sympathetic towards the French Revolution, and realized the importance of its great intellectual and political innovations. Amidst the madness of rulers and nations he upholds the project (borrowed from his master Kant) of perpetual peace and a league of nations. In a world inspired by military prowess he calls armies the ' terrible burden of mankind ', and hates the very name of war. He was not only a good European, but a good German as well, and calls on his fellow-countrymen to work for a Germany worthy of its great traditions : ' If Germany is not to become a second Poland, we must foster in every individual the feeling that we are one people, one fatherland, one language.'

It is difficult to overestimate Herder's influence, both on his time and on subsequent generations : our science, our morality, our art and our religion, and the whole of our modern civilization owe much to him. But most important of all was the great ideal he set constantly before mankind : the development and progress of the human race to an ever greater perfection, to true humanity, an ideal which can only be realized by the collective efforts of all nations led by their choicest spirits.

Half-way between Klopstock and Herder, borrowing from each but savouring still of the ' Aufklärung ', is the circle of university friends in Göttingen, which is known from this association as the ' Göttinger Dichterbund' or ' Hain'. The bardic names and the description ' Der Hain ' which they assumed, inspired by Klopstock's ode *Der Hügel und der Hain*, sufficiently show their dependence on their master. The chief members of the circle were Hölty, Miller, Voss, the brothers Stolberg, and the younger Cramer. Their organ was the *Musenalmanach*, which Boie and Gotter had edited since 1770 on the model of the French *Almanach des Muses* ; Goethe, Bürger, Leisewitz, Claudius and the brothers Jacobi, were also occasional contributors to the *Almanach*, and so stood in close connexion with this literary coterie.

Göttingen, the university town of Hanover, by its personal union with England, enjoyed a greater measure of political freedom than most other German cities, and it proved a fertile soil for the reception and propagation of nationalistic and democratic doctrines. The members of the ' Bund ' were primarily anti-French : Wieland was denounced as an arch-traitor to the cause of German nationalism; Klopstock they celebrated as the fountain-head of their inspiration, while they hailed the advent of the French Revolution with songs of liberty, and odes against tyrants. Their patriotism led them to take up with enthusiasm Herder's plea for popular poetry, and it is in this direction, and in their adaptations of foreign literature, that their chief importance lies.

The oldest and most level-headed member of the group was the Mecklenburger J. H. Voss (1751–1826). The grand-son of a serf, he was naturally the inveterate foe of tyranny in all its forms. The most permanent and artistic record of the political sympathies of this group of poets is to be found in three verse idylls dealing with the emancipation of the serfs, *Die Leibeignen, Die Erleichterten,* and *Die Freigelassenen,* based on material provided by his grandfather. But Voss had really more sympathy with the dying ' Aufklärung' than with the 'Sturm und Drang'. He has left other idylls of a realistic, thoroughly common-sense character, directly opposed to the sentimental, pseudo-classical pastorals of Gessner. The chief of these, *Luise* (1795), is still readable for its loving description of the homely background of a German household, and is still more important as having suggested to Goethe the writing of *Hermann und Dorothea.* Voss was also a somewhat uninspired translator of primitive poetry (in Herder's sense). His versions of Homer and Theocritus still rank, however, amongst the favourites of the general reading public.

The other members of the ' Göttinger Bund ' distinguished themselves mainly as lyric poets. The melancholy L. Hölty wrote tender love-songs and elegies, and mildly didactic poems of which several have found a place in every German anthology. J. M. Miller is mainly remembered by his tearful *Siegwart, eine Klostergeschichte* (1776), which out-Wertherized *Werther.* The lyrics of M. Claudius, the editor of the popular journal *Der Wandsbecker Bote,* are not unworthy forerunners of Goethe's : the famous *Abend-*

lied was rightly considered by Herder to be worthy of a place in his collection of *Volkslieder*, and other poems of Claudius are full of the same warm 'Stimmung' and delicate poetic imagery. The two Stolbergs both wrote fiery but exaggerated odes against tyrants. The elder brother, Frederick, was the more talented of the two ; but even his liberalism was not proof against the excesses of the French revolutionists, and he turned upon his former friends with a pompous ode entitled *The Huns of the West*. He finally found peace in the bosom of the Roman Church.

To the listlessness of most of the Göttingen poets G. A Bürger (1747–94) brought a spirit of energy. He was coarse and uncontrolled in his passions, and completely ruined his life by irregular matrimonial adventures. His belief in his poetic talent was almost destroyed by the sharp and one sided criticism of Schiller, who was unable to distinguish the work from the man ; nevertheless, as a poet he tower head and shoulders above his fellows, and will always be remembered as the creator of the literary ballad. Bürger had begun as an imitator of the ruder folk-song, the chief charm of which was its naïveté and grotesqueness. But under the influence of Herder's essay on *Ossian* (which contained a version of *Sweet William's Ghost*) his *Lenore* (1773) mark the transition to the new style. In the magnificent descrip tion of the ghostly ride, in which the heavens and stars over head fly past in the mad rush of the gallop, Bürger might well claim to have attained something of Shakespearian sublimity The language, a happy blend of the epic and dramatic is forcible and yet melodious, and, though occasionally exaggerated, direct and popular in tone. Within a few years, this wonderful ballad had spread from one end of Europe to the other ; nowhere was it more popular than in England where amongst its translators are numbered

Walter Scott and D. G. Rossetti. Bürger's later ballads do not reach the supreme excellence of *Lenore*. Percy's *Reliques*, which in the meanwhile had become to him as ' his morning and evening devotion', inspired him to adaptations and imitations of English ballads, such as *Der Bruder Graurock und die Pilgerin*, based on *The Friar of Orders Gray*, *Der Kaiser und der Abt* (*King John and the Abbot of Canterbury*), and *Des Pfarrers Tochter von Taubenhain*, which are not free from a certain shallow frivolity and loquacity reminiscent of the ' Bänkelsänger ' type of ballad from which he had emancipated himself in *Lenore*. Apart from *Lenore* his best ballads are *Das Lied vom braven Mann* (1777) and *Der wilde Jäger* (1778), both based on German sources. Bürger not only restored the ballad, but brought new life to the German sonnet, which had degenerated since the seventeenth century, by making its contents worthy of its noble form. It was from Bürger that A. W. Schlegel, who had sat at his feet as a student at Göttingen, learned the difficult art of sonnet-making.

Bürger also planned many translations : that from the English of the *Adventures of the Baron von Münchhausen* is still a household book in Germany and, indeed, on the Continent generally ; a version of the *Iliad* remained unfinished.

By virtue of his egotism, his glorification of instinct and passion, his aggressive radicalism, Bürger forms a fitting transition to the ' Sturm und Drang '.

V

GOETHE AND THE
'STURM UND DRANG'

WHEN Goethe came under Herder's influence in Strasbourg as a young student in 1770, he had not progressed
very far beyond the general intellectual movement of the day.
In 1749, the date of Goethe's birth, the ' Aufklärung ' was
still supreme. Goethe's father, with his strictly unemotional
views of life, was its embodiment, and exerted an influence
which was only partially counteracted by the impulsive
affection and somewhat vague religious propensities of his
mother. The most impressionable years of his boyhood had
been spent in Frankfort, occupied for a time by French
troops ; his chief source of intellectual stimulus was the
theatre set up by them. Such artistic training as he had
undergone under his father's eye in the rambling, com-
fortable house of the Grosser Hirschgraben was inspired
either by French or Italian models. In Leipzig, the ' klein
Paris ', where he remained from 1765 to 1768, ostensibly
studying at the university, the atmosphere was, in spite of
Lessing's efforts, chiefly French. Goethe responded to this
influence with two plays in alexandrines, one a pastoral
drama, *Die Laune des Verliebten* (1768), and the second, *Die
Mitschuldigen* (1769), a comedy of intrigue in an unsavoury
environment. The former play affords an early instance
of his tendency to transmute his experiences into poetical
images, which led him to speak of all his works as ' fragments
of a great confession '. ' Der Verliebte ' was Goethe him-

self, and the play sets forth his amorous dallying with Käthchen Schönkopf, an innkeeper's daughter with whose affections he trifled, and who punished him by accepting the addresses of a more serious lover. She, too, is the acknowledged inspirer of a MS. collection of lyrics, *Annette*, Leipzig 1767, of which but one was deemed by Goethe worthy of a place in the *Neue Lieder* published in 1769. Most of these, indeed, are in the prevailing anacreontic style ; it is in very few of these songs, half a dozen at the most (Goethe included nine in his collected works), that real passion emerges from the artificiality of conventional gallantry.

Goethe's dissolute student life in Leipzig had seriously impaired his health, and he was obliged, before resuming his studies, to undergo a rest-cure at home. This period of his life was of considerable importance for the enrichment of his nature with new motives and ideals. A relative of his mother's, Fräulein von Klettenberg, afterwards to re-appear in *Wilhelm Meister* in the *Confessions of a Beautiful Soul*, turned his thoughts to the inner life, and back to the Christian virtues ; and with her religion this lady combined a mystic belief in the occult powers of nature, which sent him to the study of alchemy and cabalistic speculations, that were to find expression in the first fragments of *Faust*. When finally he left Frankfort early in 1770 to resume his legal studies at Strasbourg it was considerably chastened in spirit and with a less unbalanced view of life ; he was in that frame of mind which is most receptive of new impressions and ideas.

In his autobiography Goethe holds that his acquaintance with Herder and his love for Friederike Brion were the two most important results of his stay in Strasbourg. He was at once attracted by Herder's strong personality and his individual and original outlook, and even, contrary to his wont, bore patiently the sarcasm which the elder poet levelled at his enthusiasms and fancies. The few weeks during which he sat at the master's feet wrought an entire change in his intellectual outlook, and completed the revulsion of feeling and taste which had already been maturing in Frankfort. If Goethe had already discovered for himself that Shakespeare was not the ' barbarian' Voltaire made him out to be, he now learnt to see in him the greatest of creative artists. Those qualities in Shakespeare which Herder had determined and explained objectively, Goethe felt subjectively. His short but spirited *Shakespeare-Rede* (delivered in October 1771) is a personal confession of the enormous influence that the English poet exerted on him. It is the creative spirit of the artist in Shakespeare which Goethe instinctively makes his own. In Shakespeare he found the solution of the opposition between nature and art—here was purer, more primitive nature than even in Ossian and the folk-song, and an art (as Lessing had implied) at least the equal of the art of the Greeks. Moreover Shakespeare had this advantage over the Greeks, that his characters were the incorporation of the modern world, and, as such, throbbing with living, actual impulses. Hamlet is essentially a modern hero, whose descendant in the direct line is Werther.

It is undeniable that this new conception of poetry as the artistic embodiment of the whole animate, moving, inexhaustible world of man Goethe owed to Herder and, through him, to Shakespeare. The new influence is definitely noticeable in the lyric poetry which Goethe now wrote under the inspiration of his love for the daughter of the pastor of Sesenheim. While his first lyrics to Friederike (*Balde seh' ich Rickchen wieder ; Kleine Blumen, kleine Blätter*) are not so far removed from the earlier anacreontic effusions of Leipzig, the Sesenheim poems soon betray, as a direct consequence of the meeting with Herder, a primitive intensity and a directness of passion which was new in German literature. In the songs *Willkommen und Abschied* and *Das Mailied* there is a fusion of nature with feeling which is entirely different from the reflective musings of former poets. Antiquity and the Renaissance considered the world as a developed state ; Goethe, in the wake of Herder, expressed it as a living organism. The consciousness of man's oneness with nature, that he is but part and parcel of the whole, which is ever changing, moving, developing, that poetry itself is but one of the many forms of the creative impulse, all this is present in Goethe's new lyrics. They are themselves movement, not only through the animation of material objects ('der Mond sah kläglich ') or the visualization of abstract conceptions ('goldene Träume')—this much Goethe would have found in Shakespeare or, indeed, in any great poetry—but where former poets were content with adjectival epithets, Goethe uses a present participle, as if he could only conceive of attributes as motion : ' schwebende Sterne, türmende Ferne.' Hence the numerous verbs of growing and becoming which are an essential part of Goethe's early diction : ' weben, quellen, wirken, streben,' &c. The poet's feelings broke with the conventionalities of form as well as of diction : he either returns to the simplicity of the *Volkslied* or uses the ' vers libres ' which Klopstock had introduced, without, like his model, adhering to the formal structure of the ode. As a result even the smallest of his poems has a range and variety of melody such as no lyric poetry in the world had hitherto possessed.

One of the chief reasons why Strasbourg had been chosen for the completion of his academic studies was the attraction of French culture, for which his whole upbringing, and especially his admiration for Wieland, had already given him a predilection. But he became instead the founder and leader of the national movement of the ' Sturm und Drang '. It was a similar transformation to that which Herder had undergone in France, and no doubt Herder's influence must not be left out of account. From the manifestation of the ' esprit gaulois ', as represented in its quintessence in Voltaire, Goethe turned rather to the robust individualism of Rousseau and Diderot ; the fact that they were the subjects of violent hostility in their own country rather endeared them to him. For the French ' esprit ' or ' wit ' he substituted the ' genius ' of Young ; to the uniformity of French taste he opposed the vigour of natural sentiment ; to the regularity of French pseudo-classical architecture, the splendid individuality of the Strasbourg cathedral, 'this characteristic German art ' ; in place of the conventions and restrictions of polite society he advocated the ease and freedom of natural relationships. And at the students' mess where he took his midday meal Goethe found a number of young men who eagerly imbibed the revolutionary theories which he expounded to them. Several of these, notably Lenz, Wagner, Stilling, were to make a name for themselves in literature. Many of these theories had already been put into practice by the ' Göttinger Dichterbund ', who, indeed, foreshadow the ' Sturm und Drang ' in more than one respect. But whereas the former found the lyric best suited to their somewhat elegiac mood, the latter could only find expression for their passionate restlessness in the drama. Indeed, the name of the movement is taken from the title of one of Klinger's most turbulent tragedies, *Der Wirrwarr oder Sturm und Drang* (1776). It has superseded the contemporary designation of ' Geniezeit ', because it represents more adequately the spirit of bustling energy which pervades these productions, with their constant scene-shifting, their jerkiness of diction, their exaggerations and rhetorical outbursts, their extravagant use of exclamation-marks, apostrophes, and dashes.

The 'Sturm und Drang' in its productive aspect (theoretically it starts in 1767 with Herder's *Fragmente*) may be said to date from the publication of *Götz von Berlichingen* in 1773. It virtually came to an end with Schiller's *Don Carlos* in 1787. The fact that it was dominated by the two great personalities of Goethe and Schiller renders it one of the most important movements in German literature.

The Strasbourg period, important as it was for Goethe's literary development, was a period of incubation rather than of actual production ; it was not until he returned to Frankfort that the numerous plans and sketches conceived in the shadow of the Minster were carried to fruition. The four years spent at home 1771–5 are for productiveness unparalleled in the career of any poet.

Under Herder's guidance Goethe had learned to see in Shakespeare's plays the clash of personalities, of the pretended freedom of will with the inevitable course of the world. All his productions of this period, his *Götz*, *Prometheus*, *Mahomet*, are variations of this conflict. According as to whether the influence of Shakespeare or Pindar predominated, so the form in which he clothed his titans was dramatic or epic-lyric.

In choosing the robber-knight Götz von Berlichingen as the hero of his dramatized chronicle (1773), Goethe was attracted first and foremost by the tragedy of the strong individual, the titanic personality (the ' Kerl ' as the ' Sturm und Drang ' called him) in conflict with the anarchical forces of his time. But there was also the nationalistic, popular element in the story which appealed to him for itself. Eventually the visualizing of the time of the action, the description of the virile, matter-of-fact, thoroughly realistic sixteenth century, the local colour, absorbed his interest more and more, until he aimed finally at creating for Germany, what Shakespeare had done in his 'histories' for England, a dramatic record of national greatness. Hence the magnificent background of knighthood and peasantry, emperor and priesthood, Holy 'Vehme' and Reformation, which pass as a rapid succession of tableaux, and which really overshadow the personality of the hero. And it was this aspect of the drama which appealed primarily to his contemporaries, for *Götz* is at the fountain-head of a host of 'Ritterstücke', in which the costumes and scenic effects were the main attraction. To some extent, no doubt, *Götz* is also a 'confession' : it is agreed that, in meting out poetical justice to Weislingen for his betrayal of Götz's gentle sister Maria, Goethe was drawing on his own experiences at Sesenheim. But neither this pair of lovers, nor the amours of Adelheid, form an integral part of the drama : Adelheid, especially, is not really drawn from nature, her literary ancestry, her relationship to Cleopatra, to Marwood, to the Gräfin Orsina, is too obvious.

Herder's criticism of *Götz*—'Shakespeare has quite spoiled you '—referred in the first place to the looseness of the construction. For, dramaturgically, *Götz* is a monstrosity ; in the third act alone the scene changes no less than nineteen times, and each of these scenes, though constituting a unity in itself, stands in no inevitable relationship to the whole. In his endeavours to copy the fulness of life, which he found in his model, Goethe missed the fact that, though his methods might be different, Shakespeare's dramas were centred just as strictly round a great character or passion as any of Racine's or Lessing's. But the very elements which went to make *Götz* a success—the ardour and tenderness of the feeling, the vindication of German nationalism, the rush of movement, the swing of its diction—proved the undoing of lesser poets, who, while copying and exaggerating its licence, failed to catch its spirit of creative enthusiasm. For it is the poetic revival and glorification of a whole period of national life that assures for *Götz von Berlichingen* a permanent place in German literature.

In his attempts to revive poetically the sixteenth century, Goethe was attracted by another great romantic figure, that of Faust, the scholar-magician, which was to haunt him for the rest of his life. While there is little enough of the ' Titan ' in the historical charlatan of the first *Volksbuch von Dr. Faust* of 1587, the character had already undergone a certain ennoblement at the hands of Marlowe. And though Marlowe's *Dr. Faustus* (1590) did not become known to Goethe until 1818, much of its spirit had passed into the Faust dramas of the strolling English players, who roamed Germany in the seventeenth century, and through them into the puppet shows, the oldest of which goes back to 1604. Lessing, moreover, by his fragment in the *Literaturbriefe*, had raised Faust to literary dignity. Here, then, was a figure after Goethe's own heart, whom he could invest with his own passionate desire for life, with the same striving to concentrate in his own personality the infinite variety of the universe. The conflict between these two forces, that which bids a man live his life to the full, and that which urges him to neglect the joys of the senses for those of the spirit, the fight between the real and the ideal, is at the root of the *Faust* tragedy, because it is the symbol of Goethe's own existence—he too was conscious of the ' two souls within his breast ' ; he too, like Faust, had experienced the futility of knowledge, and returned dissatisfied from the ways of life. But we must beware of exaggerating the philosophic background of *Faust*, at least of the *Urfaust*, as it existed during these early Strasbourg and Frankfort days, and of which a record, incomplete though it may be, has been preserved in the copy made by Fräulein von Göchhausen, and discovered in 1885. It is here only the first monologue : 'Habe nun, ach! Philosophie,' which contains any hint of the problem to be unravelled later in the *Erster Theil* of 1808. With the scenes between Mephistopheles and the student and the ' Auerbachs Keller ' episode—in which Faust himself and not the devil practises his hocus-pocus—the *Urfaust* passes without transition to the Gretchen tragedy, which is complete in its chief particulars. There is as yet only a suggestion as to how the lacuna, the ' grosse Lücke ', is to be filled and the introduction of Mephistopheles brought about. The *Urfaust* is primarily the human tragedy of Faust's love for, and betrayal of, the simple burgher maiden, who is painted with some of the traits of Friederike Brion. Goethe unfolds the fate of the two lovers, from the charming idyll of the opening scenes to the pathos of the prison, with a tragic power which is weakened by none of the retarding digressions of the completed work, and which artistically makes the *Urfaust* a much more satisfying drama than the *First Part*. And, apart from its tragic intensity, the *Urfaust* contains the major portion of those supremely poetical lines and passages which we have come to associate with the quintessence of Goethe's worldly wisdom.

If *Faust* is the crowning poetic achievement of Goethe's youthful genius, *Die Leiden des jungen Werther* (1774) was its most popular manifestation. In 1772 Goethe, at his father's instance, had spent four months in Wetzlar in order to gain some practical insight into the functions of the supreme court of justice of the empire. Among his new friends were Kestner and his betrothed, Charlotte Buff, with whom the impressionable Goethe was soon violently in love. But Lotte, a prudent, essentially practically-minded young

woman, was proof against the seductive young genius, and
after a bitter struggle Goethe tore himself away from
Wetzlar.   Another equally absorbing passion for Maxi-
miliane von Laroche, who became the wife of the Frankfort
merchant Brentano, seemed destined for a moment to termi-
nate less harmoniously ; but here, too, the jealous husband
was eventually conciliated.   Shortly after he left Wetzlar an
indelible impression had been made on Goethe, in the state of
passionate, sentimental emotion in which he then was, by the
suicide of young Jerusalem, who had taken his life out of
hopeless love for the wife of a colleague.   But it was not only
these personal experiences which went to make up *Werther*,
not merely the ' taedium vitae ' which had caused Goethe
for a time to dally with the thought of self-destruction ; there
were also important literary factors.   The ' Weltschmerz ' of
Werther is born not only of the consciousness of the disproportion between the real and the ideal in Goethe's own
breast, but is typical of the melancholy of a whole period.   It
had been prepared by the tearfulness of the *Night Thoughts* of
Young, by the idyllic atmosphere of Goldsmith, by the
sentimentalism of Sterne, the tenderness of Richardson, by
the mournful haziness of *Ossian*, and, above all, by the
nature-philosophy of Rousseau.   The result was a state
of discontent with existing conditions and environment
which engendered restlessness and pessimism.   Such ' Weltschmerz ' is obviously present in a lesser or greater degree in
every human being at all periods of history, but towards the
end of the eighteenth century it became almost epidemic.
The unsatisfactory state of political and social conditions
in Germany led the cultured classes to morbid depression.
Goethe's *Werther* is thus the tragedy of a noble individual,
for whom ' the times are out of joint ', who through intense
retrospection and excessive brooding over real and fancied

wrongs loses all self-control, and suffers complete moral and physical shipwreck. And Goethe has analysed his hero's disease—for such excessive morbidity is a disease—with a photographic fidelity which renders *Werthers Leiden* the first of our modern pathological novels. The letter-form, which Goethe adopted from Richardson and Rousseau, itself gives an impression of realism. Several of the letters in *Werther* look like verbal transcripts of Goethe's or Kestner's; next to the dramatic, with which it has, at least, the dialogue in common, it was the form which best kept up the tension of the reader. It combines, as no other ' genre ' can, the epic and the lyric, and renders the sudden transition into the narrative of Werther's death the more effective.

Werther, moreover, represents the struggle for nature and freedom, the revolt against rules and conventions, against empty formalism and indifference, whether in life, education, or art : it is a glorification of human nature. It is characterized, in accordance with Rousseau's teaching, by the love of the natural, unspoiled people of the soil, and especially of children; the many descriptions of patriarchal conditions and homely incidents are worthy of the naïveté of *Hermann und Dorothea*, and the love of nature finds expression in the reaction of the hero to her changing moods. The happiness of the first part reflects the sunny atmosphere of Homer, while the pessimism of the second drives the hero to the gloomy, misty world of Ossian. All this was a revelation to an age still steeped in stiffness and affectation ; the times were ripe, and the book let loose a flood of sentimentality which threatened to swamp the common-sense of Europe. Translations, imitations, parodies appeared in every European language, and at one stroke Goethe established an international reputation as ' the elegant author of *The Sorrows of Werther* ', which was his chief title to European fame for the next fifty years.

The theme of the unfaithful lover which Goethe had treated in the Weislingen and Maria episode in *Götz* and in the Gretchen tragedy of *Faust* found further expression in yet another dramatic confession, *Clavigo*, published a few months before *Werther* in 1774. Fired by the adverse criticism levelled against the formlessness of *Götz*, Goethe was determined to show that he could, if he chose, write a play which should conform strictly with the rules of the theatre. It was not in vain that he had schooled himself on *Emilia Galotti* : the action is thoroughly logical, tense and technically flawless ; there are no digressive episodes, the individual characters are raised to types, and the scenes are built up in careful contrast. Yet, in spite of its theatrical effectiveness, *Clavigo* does not impress the reader as a great work, possibly because the hero, with his Werther-like irresolution and lack of character, has not strength enough to sustain the action. Posterity has endorsed the disappointment of Goethe's friends that he should have turned his back upon the splendid vigour of *Götz*. The chief interest of *Clavigo* is the revelation of himself in the hero, and especially in the matter-of-fact Carlos, some of whose speeches strike a very modern note.

After *Götz* and *Werther* Goethe was the poet of the hour, and his reputation procured him the entrée into circles to which neither his birth nor his fortune would otherwise have admitted him. It was thus that he became acquainted with the Frankfort patrician family of the Schönemanns, the widow and daughter of a rich banker. Most of the women Goethe had loved hitherto had been both socially and intellectually his inferiors ; here in Lili Schönemann was a woman, rich, beautiful, well-educated, accustomed to flattery and adulation, and rather inclined to look upon her lover as an eccentric young poet. Goethe was alternately attracted by her charm and repelled by her surroundings ; she was an inhabitant of that rococo world of polite insincerity and affectedness which he thought he had left behind in Leipzig. But eventually an understanding, a half engagement, was arranged between them which only served to arouse in Goethe his old aversion to the bonds of matrimony. Some of the great lyrics of this period : *Neue Liebe, neues Leben ; An Belinden,* present us with a picture of his conflicting emotions, torn as he was between his longing for Lili and his desire for the fullest self-expression, which marriage must inevitably check. To one of his anonymous admirers, the Countess Auguste von Stolberg, with whom he kept up a most intimate correspondence, Goethe poured out the emotions and the passion with which Lili inspired him. It was in this frame of mind that he wrote *Stella* (1776) with the significant sub-title *Ein Schauspiel für Liebende.* ' Unless I wrote dramas I should perish ! ' he wrote to Auguste, and, as these words suggest, *Stella* is one of the most subjective portraits he has given us. His hero Fernando is torn between his love for two women, each of whom he has abandoned in turn, and ends by taking them both to his bosom as Goethe had done, in his thoughts at least, with Lili and Auguste. He represented to himself the ideal woman in the combination of the poetic, romantic Stella with the serious, high-minded Cäcilie. But Goethe was not much concerned with the problem of the play, the bigamy motif being after all but the symbol of the state of fluctuation of mind and vacillation of purpose which his relations with Lili had induced. It was consequently a matter of comparative indifference to him to alter, at Schiller's instance, the typical ' Sturm und Drang ' solution into a conventionally tragic ending. That *Stella* is so effective on the stage is not due to the characters—Fernando is mood rather than will—but to the careful attention to dramatic technique : the unity of time, for instance, is strictly observed. The appeal of the play is proved, moreover, by the numerous imitations and translations which appeared on all hands. In England it contributed, with *Werther* and *Faust*, to establish for Goethe a reputation of immorality from which, even to-day, he has not wholly recovered.

The two operettas of this period, *Erwin und Elmire* and *Claudine von Villa Bella*, afford, after *Stella*, the best commentary on his love for Lili. The fact that they both go back in their inspiration to that conventional atmosphere, which he had treated as a raw youth in the *Laune des Verliebten*, is a sufficient testimony to the enormous influence which the fashionable patrician lady exerted on the young ' Stürmer und Dränger '.

The arrival in Frankfort of the two Counts Stolberg with a proposal that Goethe should accompany them on a tour to Switzerland was very welcome as an escape from the intolerable situation in which he found himself with regard to his betrothed. It afforded him the opportunity of visiting his sister Cornelie, who, out of the wisdom of her own unhappy marriage, used all her influence to dissuade him from the union with Lili. While he was away, similar arguments were urged by Lili's relations, who had always been averse to the match. Finally the engagement was broken off by mutual consent. But, although free, Goethe was not happy. The memory of Lili still haunted him even amid the bustle and excitement of the early years in Weimar, until it was finally effaced by the new love for Frau von Stein. But his affection for Lili was sufficiently strong for him to declare fifty years later that she was the one and only woman he had really loved.

As usual with him, he turned for consolation to poetry. The inspiration of *Egmont* and its first acts belongs to the last few months in Frankfort, although it was not published until after his return from Italy. The plan of the tragedy may even go back to Strasbourg days when, in his study of the sixteenth century, the figure of Egmont would have appealed to him as an apostle of freedom similar to Götz.

Egmont is the symbol of Goethe's fatalism, that belief in what he called 'das Dämonische', that mysterious, inexplicable power within the breast of man, which, in opposition to all the dictates of moral order and reason, urges him irresistibly onwards, now to fame and now to destruction. Ever since Goethe had escaped the fate he had just depicted in his *Werther* he was obsessed with an unshakable faith in his destiny. But it would at first sight appear strange that he should have discovered in the historical Egmont the child of circumstances which he felt himself to be at this time. And in order to do so he was obliged to modify historical facts to a considerable extent. The real Egmont was a middle-aged man, the father of eleven children, with a strong sense of duty to his family and his country. Goethe pictured him as a young man, of about his own age, unmarried, unfettered by any family ties, but blessed with an all-absorbing love. He invested him with characteristics which he himself possessed, and emphasized others which the historical Egmont already shared with him—his unbounded enjoyment of life, his self-confidence, his power of attracting men and winning their favour and affection.

The freedom with which Goethe dealt with his hero destroyed such little dramatic action as the historical fable possessed ; and it is not until the fourth act that Egmont takes the decision of throwing in his lot with the popular cause. But even here the action is not dramatic, for Alba has resolved to arrest him, whatever the outcome of their interview. ' I was not born to be a tragic poet ', Goethe wrote to Zelter in his old age, and it was easy enough for Schiller to

show that *Egmont* runs counter to all the requirements of a
drama. The fact that it is still among the most popular of
Goethe's works is due undoubtedly to the charm of the
scenes with Clärchen. In this simple seamstress Goethe
has presented us with his ideal of unsophisticated, sensuous,
devoted womanhood, such as he found realized later in
Christiane Vulpius. But in *Egmont* her origin is negative
rather than positive ; she is drawn in direct contrast to Lili
Schönemann ; her love is sufficient unto itself, and in giving
herself body and soul to her lover she has no thought of the
marriage ties, she is not even actuated, as is Gretchen in *Faust*,
by the hope of binding him more closely to her. She is the
quintessence of eroticism, of love as satisfaction, as opposed
to love as passion, with its concomitants of jealousy and
regard for conventions.

The other characters of the play are mere foils to bring
out the various phases of Egmont's personality : in preparing
Egmont for the stage Schiller was able to leave out the Regent
and Machiavelli altogether, without their being missed. If
Egmont is the Goethe of Frankfort days, Orange is the
Goethe of Weimar, whose exuberance and frivolity have
been subdued by responsibility. In these two figures there
is already something of the contrast between Tasso and
Antonio, for *Tasso* was already occupying Goethe's thoughts
by the time *Egmont* was published in 1788. But that was a
later development, and it is essentially the young Goethe that
interests us in *Egmont*, the Goethe who broke with tradition
and family, who even sacrificed his love to the demoniac
force which drove him on when he accepted, in spite of all
the strenuous objections raised by his republican-minded
father, the invitation of Karl August, Duke of Saxe-
Weimar, to visit him, not knowing whither he went, caring
even less, only too glad to shake the dust of ' accursed

Frankfort' from off his feet. 'As if goaded by invisible spirits, the sun-steeds of time bolt with the light car of our destiny ; and nothing remains for us but, with calm self-possession, firmly to grasp the reins, and now to the right, and now to the left, to guide the wheels from the precipice here, and the rock there. Whither we are hastening, who knows ? Does any one remember whence he came ?' It was with these words from *Egmont* that Goethe most fittingly concluded his autobiography, which takes the reader only to this point of his career. With his entry into Weimar Goethe felt that a whole phase of his existence had passed, and that he had entered into an unknown future.

All the 'Sturm und Drang' dramatists who followed in Goethe's wake, Lenz, Wagner, Leisewitz, Klinger, Maler Müller, were animated by the same passionate desire for complete self-expression, the same subordination of reason to the emotions, the same revolt against all restraints, both moral and literary. But they exaggerated the purely external characteristics until these became for them the essentials— in their insistence on being natural they became coarse and revolting, and they lacked the mental and moral balance of Goethe which raised him above his creations.

Of the younger representatives of the 'Sturm und Drang' none is more characteristic both of its revolutionary and of its national spirit than Schiller, and it was only natural that the cloak of leadership should fall on his shoulders as Goethe became more and more hostile to the movement.

The fact that Friedrich Schiller was born in 1759, ten years after Goethe, naturally implies in him a different outlook upon life and art. When Schiller grew into manhood German literature, under the influence of Lessing and Goethe, had taken a leap forward from the rococo affectation which still prevailed in Goethe's youth. Schiller was brought up on

Rousseau and the revolutionary doctrines of the early
' Sturm und Drang '. His first play, *Die Räuber* (1781),
written during his last years at Duke Karl Eugen's military
academy at Stuttgart, is essentially the product of these literary
influences, rather than a reflection of his revolt against the
petty tyranny he endured at that institution. The motif of
Die Räuber—hostile brothers in love with the same woman
and in conflict with their father—is amongst the most popular
in the literature of the day. But by building on an historical
background, and laying the scene in the Germany of the
Seven Years War, Schiller has invested the story with an
actuality which made even *Götz* seem old-fashioned. The
greatness and importance of *Die Räuber* consists in the
faithful picture it presents of the thoughts of an age. Karl
Moor is the individualist, the ' sublime criminal ' whom
Rousseau had extolled ; he is also the sentimentalist, the
man of feeling, as opposed to Franz, the rationalist, the
materialist, the cynic. Between them the two brothers
personified the forces which were to come into such violent
conflict a few years later in the French Revolution. The
whole play, in its denunciation of the tyranny of princes and of
established society, breathes the spirit of revolt, and it furnished
admirable political propaganda for the French Jacobins, as it
does still to-day for the Russian Bolsheviks. The motto ' In
tirannos ! ', although not directly due to Schiller, seemed in
itself to warrant the action of the Assemblée Législative in
granting to Schiller a diploma of French citizenship.

But *Die Räuber* is more than a revolutionary play : it is
first and foremost the tragedy of a noble soul. In Karl Moor,
the Titan, the exponent of impossible ideals, the rebel against
the empty forms of society, the would-be saviour of mankind,
we have a tragic figure of the first magnitude. His greatness
lies not so much in the hopeless battle he wages with society

as in the conflict in his own breast. The sublime idea of reforming the world single-handed is tempered by the knowledge that the means he uses are despicable ; he recognizes all too late the futility of his aims and that ' two men such as he would destroy the whole moral edifice of the world '.

The dramatic power of *Die Räuber* is unquestionable—to-day it can hold an audience as no other play of Schiller's can —it has scenes of unforgettable beauty and grandeur, such as that on the banks of the Danube, or that in the forest at old Moor's dungeon. One willingly forgives Schiller the youthful exaggerations and bombast, the improbabilities, the faults against good taste, the unreality of some of the characters. The dramatic action is intense, the concentration of time and place truly remarkable. In the somewhat mellowed version prepared by Schiller for the Mannheim stage it took the theatrical world by storm : ' If ever we may expect a German Shakespeare, then this is the man ', wrote one of the most discerning critics of the day, and extravagant as this praise may appear, it is undeniable that with *Die Räuber* German tragedy entered on a new stage of development. It established Schiller's reputation as a dramatist, not only at home, but throughout Europe, and both in France and in England it was almost as popular as it was in Germany.

The triumphant performance of *Die Räuber* on the Mannheim stage in 1782 marked the turning-point of Schiller's career. Life as a regimental doctor now seemed unbearable, and he longed to devote himself to literature. A youthful escapade brought upon him the displeasure of his sovereign ; an offence which a reference in *Die Räuber* was alleged to have given to a Swiss canton incensed the Duke still more, and brought the order to ' write no more comedies on the pain of instant dismissal '. Schiller's answer was to seek liberty and safety in flight.

After many bitter disappointments he received a temporary appointment as dramatic poet at Mannheim. Under his contract he was required to provide three new plays ; one of these, *Fiesco*, was already finished when he left Stuttgart, and after a complete revision was produced at Mannheim in 1784. This ' republican tragedy ', in spite of many fine scenes, is inferior to *Die Räuber*. The reason lies less in the treatment than in the unsatisfactory nature of the hero. To Rousseau, Fiesco, Count of Lavagna, appealed as a noble criminal whose conspiracy against the rule of the Dorias in Genoa was inspired solely by his love of the republican institutions. This view seemed supported by the *Conjuration du Comte de Fiesque* of Cardinal de Retz, and it was as such that he appealed primarily to Schiller, as Karl Moor had appealed to him, through his moral greatness. But reference to more serious historians like Robertson proved Fiesco to have been more of a Catiline than a Brutus, his incentive being ambition rather than republican zeal. The chief weakness of *Fiesco* lies in Schiller's vacillation between these two conceptions of his hero's character. Whereas it had been easy enough to endow Karl Moor, his creation, with his own somewhat vague political enthusiasms, he found it well nigh impossible to fasten them on to the historical Fiesco. The result is the complete inconsistency of the hero's character, which made it possible for Schiller to substitute a happy for a tragic ending, thus proving that there was no real dramatic necessity for either. As a stage play, however, *Fiesco* marks a distinct advance on *Die Räuber* ; in this respect *Emilia Galotti*, from which the Verrina-Bertha episode is copied, proved a valuable model. The intrigue is worked out with great skill, certain scenes are of great theatrical effect, and one character at least, that of the rascally Moor, Muley Hassan, is perfectly consistent and endowed with a sense of humour which is rare in Schiller. Moreover *Fiesco* occupies an important place in Schiller's dramatic development as the first step in the direction of the grand historical tragedy.

Kabale und Liebe, ein bürgerliches Trauerspiel (1784), was Schiller's second instalment in fulfilment of his contract with the Mannheim stage. It was conceived and written almost simultaneously with *Fiesco*, but is undoubtedly superior to that drama. Such an actual subject from common life was both more congenial to him and more in keeping with his training than the ' haute tragédie ' he had attempted in *Fiesco*. Once more it was Rousseau who, if he did not actually furnish the subject, provided the spirit of the drama. The *Nouvelle Héloïse*, with its moralizing tale of the unhappy love of the baron's daughter for the bourgeois St. Preux, formed a welcome thesis for several dramatists of the ' Sturm und Drang '. Wagner and Lenz had each treated the motif in an unsavoury tragedy ; Otto von Gemmingen had taken up the theme again from Diderot's *Père de Famille*, but had given it a happy ending. It had long been present to Schiller's mind and he had used it episodically both in *Die Räuber* and in *Fiesco*. Apart from these literary influences there is also much that is personal in the play ; Schiller was consumed with the same pangs of jealousy as Ferdinand through his unrequited love for the daughter of his benefactress, Frau von Wolzogen. The social background is a faithful reproduction of the conditions prevailing at the corrupt and licentious court of Wirtemberg with its rule of mistresses and its trade in mercenaries. That the figure of the musician Miller is so admirable and lifelike is due, no doubt, to his being very largely modelled on Schiller's father.

Technically, *Kabale und Liebe* is admittedly a masterpiece. Once more Schiller had profited much from *Emilia Galotti* ; the time of the action takes barely two days, there are no

superfluous characters, no digressions ; the style, too, shows
a marked improvement ; there is less bombast, more simple,
natural dialogue, and, above all, the characters, even the
women characters, are less shadowy, less unreal than in the
former plays.   Here was a great advance on the formless,
brutal, biassed productions of the 'Sturm und Drang'.   In
Kabale und Liebe the love element is certainly stronger than
the intrigue ; the play is, indeed, one of the few outstanding
love tragedies of the eighteenth century.   The scenes from
family life are drawn with a poetic fidelity which makes the
atmosphere of the drama truly national, as the plays of
Shakespeare are national.   In *Kabale und Liebe* Schiller was
on the way to transform the tragedy of common life, with its
social and moralizing aims, into a genuine tragedy of human
fate.   That these promising beginnings were never fulfilled,
that the intrigue of *Fiesco* predominated again in Schiller's
next work, *Don Carlos,* marks a critical point in the German
drama.

As planned by Schiller during the Bauerbach period *Don
Carlos* was a pendant to *Kabale und Liebe* : it was to be a
'family tragedy' in a royal house, the pivot of the drama
being the love between the prince and his stepmother, with
a similar background of court cabals and intrigues.   The
prince was to have been a counterpart of Ferdinand, or, as
Schiller wrote to Reinwald, ' with the soul from Shakespeare's
Hamlet, blood and nerves from Leisewitz, and the pulse from
me.'   But, during the year spent as theatre poet in Mannheim, Schiller's views underwent a great transformation, and
with them his conception of *Don Carlos*.   In natural reaction
against the excesses of the 'Sturm und Drang', the literary
circles centring round the ' Deutsche Gesellschaft ', to which
Schiller himself belonged, favoured a return to the French
drama, a necessity which Wieland had of late urged with

great insistence. In suggesting the subject to him Dalberg, the director of the Mannheim theatre, may himself have had a similar aim. It was a theme reminiscent of *Phèdre* with all the requirements of ' haute tragédie ', its royal personages, its ' grande passion ' and its remoteness of subject-matter. The plays of Otway and Campistron which Schiller consulted, and which, like his own, were based on St. Réal's story, served to intensify his tendency towards the classical drama. Schiller admits in a letter to Dalberg that he had sought inspiration from the works of the great French dramatists, but that he hoped in *Don Carlos* to maintain the equilibrium between English and French tastes.

As time progressed and *Don Carlos* remained unfinished, the balance inclined more and more to the French style. The study of the *Hamburgische Dramaturgie* failed to convince Schiller that Voltaire was wrong in principle, though he might not be right in details. And when under the influence of *Nathan der Weise* and Wieland's *Lady Johanna Gray*, and especially of the dramatist F. W. Gotter, an active supporter of the Voltairean tragedy, he determined to recast *Don Carlos* in verse, the latinization was complete.

With the change of form went a transformation of spirit ; from a love tragedy *Don Carlos* became a political drama with the Marquis Posa, instead of the prince, as its central figure. It is symbolical of his changing outlook that from Rousseau, the would-be destroyer of civilization, Schiller now turned to Montesquieu and his *Esprit des Lois* for the political idealism which Posa champions so strangely at the despotic court of Philip II. In fact there is still a third principal theme : that of the sentimental friendship of Carlos and Posa, modelled on that of Schiller and his new friend Körner.

Don Carlos was begun in 1782 and the first three acts appeared in the *Rheinische Thalia* in 1785, but the completed play did not come out in book form until 1787. Schiller found it impossible to weld the several conceptions into a harmonious whole, and the play abounds in inconsistencies and contradictions, which his *Briefe über Don Carlos* (1788) could do little to extenuate. The remainder of Schiller's dramatic career was, indeed, spent in the endeavour to restore the balance between the English and French ideal of tragedy, which *Don Carlos* had been unable to preserve.

Don Carlos is, however, more than a record of the series of literary theories which seized upon the poet between the years 1782 and 1783 ; it is also autobiographical and subjective like no other play of Schiller's, either before or after. The passionate love of Carlos for the Queen is a reflection of Schiller's attachment to Charlotte von Kalb, the wife of a French officer ; the relations between Carlos and Posa are based on the warm friendships of Schiller for Streicher, Reinwald and Körner, friendships which amounted almost to a cult. The yearning of Carlos to leave Madrid was symptomatic of Schiller's desire to escape from Mannheim, overwhelmed as he was by debts and disappointments. Deliverance came to Schiller in the shape of an invitation by four fervent unknown admirers to Leipzig and, later, to Dresden. With one of these, C. G. Körner, the acquaintanceship ripened into a lifelong friendship, and after Schiller's migration to Weimar the letters to Körner form the most valuable commentary on his poetic activities.

VI

THE RETURN TO CLASSICISM

WHEN in November 1775 Goethe drove into Weimar, ostensibly on a short visit to the young reigning duke, it would have been difficult to foresee that this petty capital of a petty duchy would hold a young genius seething with energy for the remainder of his days. At first sight, indeed, there was not much to attract a young poet fresh from the triumphs of authorship ; the town itself was little more than an overgrown village, its atmosphere was that of drowsy provincialism, its environs could not compare with those of Frankfort, and, apart from Wieland, there was no promise of intellectual companionship.   In other respects, however, Weimar offered very strong inducements in the social opportunities it afforded ; as the bosom friend of the Duke, Goethe became intimately acquainted with an aristocratic order of society which then stood for culture ; he could acquire and practise those arts and graces of life for which his intercourse with the fashionable daughter of the Frankfort banker had given him a taste.   Goethe all his life showed a deep reverence for the manners that ' makyth man ', and his social ideals were essentially those of the ' ancien régime ' under which he was born.   When after the first few months of wild and riotous living the Duke offered him a seat on his council and a responsible post in his government, Goethe felt that his material existence was assured in a way which allowed him full bent for the exercise of all his powers and promised the fullest development of his personality.

For a time, indeed, there had been the danger that his great talents would run to waste in the trivialities and dissipations of the court. But the ever increasing responsibilities of his official duties directed his boundless energy into more fruitful channels, and from Dr. Goethe, the merry-maker and 'maître de plaisir' of a frivolous court he became von Goethe, the privy councillor and all-powerful minister of state. It may be questioned, however, whether the intensely practical life which he now led, the wider outlook on life which he gained from his commerce with men and their works, were as beneficial for his poetry as some of his biographers have pretended ; the fact remains that the first ten years spent in Weimar were almost barren of poetic results. Apart from the delicate one-act play *Die Geschwister* (1776), and the lyrics inspired by Frau von Stein, the harvest of these years comprises only some ephemeral comic operas, a satire in imitation of Aristophanes' *Birds*, and *Der Triumph der Empfindsamkeit*, in which he mocks at that sentimentality which he had done so much to foster by his *Werther*. The numerous fragments which he brought with him from Frankfort remained uncompleted, and for neither *Tasso* nor *Iphigenie* could he as yet find a suitable form. One work of this period, however, deserves more than a passing mention, if only because of the valuable insight it affords into his mental growth. *Wilhelm Meisters Theatralische Sendung* (1777–85), discovered by a lucky chance at Zürich in 1909, is the finest imaginative production of these ten years of literary fallowness. It has more of the directness, the naïveté, the strength and freshness of youth than the *Lehrjahre*, to which it stands in much the same relation as the *Urfaust* to the completed work. The *Sendung* is particularly valuable, as the expression of a distinct artistic epoch of Goethe's poetry : the period in which Shakespeare and the theatre represented to him the symbol of the world, the quintessence of an age. Wilhelm Meister is filled with the desire of founding a national theatre, which should succeed where Gottsched, Ekhof and Schröder had failed. This is the 'Sendung' which causes him to give up the certainty of a bourgeois existence and throw in his lot with a typical eighteenth-century company of strolling players. In Wilhelm's relation to the actors and actresses we have the reflection of Goethe's attitude to society. The sympathy with which he follows their fortunes, while retaining independence of mind and judgement, the contrast of the Bohemian world of the theatre with the aristocratic society of the castle, the pettiness and squabbles to which he rises superior, all this serves to build Wilhelm's character and to prepare him for the time when, as in the completed *Meister*, he will be able to turn his back upon the stage to play his part in the larger theatre of life. For even in the *Urmeister* the change of motive is visible : Wilhelm's decision to become an actor does not, we feel, carry finality with it, and there are hints of a sequel in which Wilhelm, the dilettante of art, shall become the artist of life. It was doubtless his own wavering moods, and the meditative melancholy of his own *Werther*, which inspired Goethe with that famous criticism of *Hamlet*, of the hero who sinks beneath the weight of a heavy burden, which he can neither carry nor cast off. If in one sense the *Theatralische Sendung* was on the way to become a ' Bildungsroman ', the story of a young man winning through to culture and peace with the world, it still, in two of its characters, harks back to the time when Goethe was possessed by the demoniac forces of fate. The harper incorporates the dark mysterious destiny which shapes men's lives, forces which no one can know ' who never ate his bread with tears '. Mignon's songs are the outburst of pent-up, undefined longing : *Nur wer die*

Sehnsucht kennt, weiss was ich leide; of longing for a beautiful country: *Kennst du das Land, wo die Zitronen blüh'n?* or they hint enigmatically at some dark secret of her existence: *Heiss mich nicht reden, heiss mich schweigen.* These unforgettable figures with their haunting songs contributed not a little to the popularity of *Wilhelm Meister*, and were a great source of inspiration to the Romanticists.

Goethe's first few years in Weimar were not without their disappointments and rebuffs, and he was many times on the point of throwing up his official appointments and regaining his freedom. That he was prevailed upon to stay almost against his will was entirely due to a new attraction, to the influence of Frau von Stein. She was the wife of a court dignitary, the mother of several children, of a good Scottish family on her mother's side, and had been brought up from childhood in the atmosphere of the court. She was the embodiment of social distinction and practical common-sense, and a woman of a type very different from those Goethe had hitherto loved. Although the erotic element was not wanting in his relations to her, and she often had to moderate his transports, yet it was the spirit, rather than the body, that he loved in her. She became to him the ideal of harmony, of purity, of the moral sense :

> Willst du genau erfahren was sich ziemt ?
> So frage nur bei edlen Frauen an,

is Goethe's acknowledgement in *Tasso* of his debt to her. She soon became the confidante of his troubles and aspirations, of his whims and fancies ; he wrote to her several times a day, wonderful letters, which are among the great things in the world's literature, for they lay bare a poet's soul. That Frau von Stein may not have been the high-souled woman her lover imagined her to be, is really immaterial ; the question can hardly be settled, for Goethe returned her letters and she destroyed them.   But she will continue to live in literature as he has immortalized her, the personification of the ideal which inspired his life and poetry for the space of ten years .

Under her sympathetic influence the heaven-storming defiance of his youth gradually passed into the mature calm induced by wise moderation and self-control.   It was in this sense that, next to Shakespeare, Goethe calls ' Lida ' (the name by which she goes in his poetry) the greatest formative influence on his life : ' Lida! Glück der nächsten Nähe : William ! Stern der höchsten Höhe, Euch verdank' ich was ich bin.'   And so it is that the lyrics of this period, and especially those to Frau von Stein, are rather the reflection of his spiritual evolution than of his love ; less the expression of a personal emotion than a poetical *aperçu* of a period of his life : the conviction that man should keep within the limits of the comprehensible, but within those limits should put forth his whole strength : so *An meine Bäume, Der du von dem Himmel bist, Warum gabst du uns die tiefen Blicke ?, Trost in Tränen, Hoffnung, Erinnerung, Grenzen der Menschheit, Das Göttliche.*   In most of these poems, too (that entitled *An den Mond* is a notable exception), Goethe's attitude to nature has undergone a change.   He no longer ' feels ' nature as the living organism pulsating to his own thoughts and reflections ; the landscape is now external to man, indifferent, even hostile, a frame in which to set his poetry, now no longer written about his own personality, but dealing with man as a type of humanity, as an abstract being subject to fate.   The poems *Harzreise im Winter* and *Ilmenau* are good examples of this new conception of nature as the mirror in which to reflect the fate of man.   To a large extent, no doubt, this change of attitude was brought about by Goethe's familiarity with nature, which in Weimar was now his constant environment, whereas in earlier days it had represented to him the escape from the confinement of the town. And again, from feeling nature subjectively as a poet, he had begun to study it objectively as a scientist. Such time as he could filch from official duties he devoted ardently to anatomy, botany, geology. What attracted him in science was not so much the garnering of new facts as the general principles which could be evolved from them. His discovery of the intermaxillary bone in man, thus proving man to be of the same stock as the lower animals, filled Goethe with inexpressible delight, and he already possessed a clue to his next scientific discovery, the metamorphosis of plants. It is difficult for us to realize that these scientific achievements meant more to him than his poetical talents, we have to remember that to the end of his life his interests in science never abated. That, however, amidst the practical questions of life and his absorption with science, he had not lost the art of purely naïve poetical expression is proved by the three great ballads written during this period, *Der Fischer*, *Erlkönig*, *Der Sänger*, all of them masterpieces of the super-sensuous element he had caught so well in *Der König in Thule*.

During these first ten years in Weimar Goethe had learnt self-control, and had disciplined himself by the daily routine, but it was at the cost of the free development of his genius. The pettiness of his surroundings, the burden and worries of official duties, the doubts which assailed him as to his true vocation, the lack of sympathy and understanding for his ideals of art and life, and a gradual estrangement even from Frau von Stein, all combined to make life a misery to him. It was in these circumstances that Goethe suddenly determined to seek bodily health and spiritual refreshment in the promised land of Italy.

To understand something of Goethe's passionate craving

for Italy one must realize its meaning for him, and, indeed, for the world of the eighteenth century. It was not, as it was to the Romanticists and is to the modern traveller, the land of medieval and Renaissance splendour, of historical associations. To Goethe, as it had been previously to Winckelmann and Lessing, it was, if not the cradle, at least the museum of antique art, and the best substitute for Greece itself, at that time still under the heel of the Turk. For Goethe in particular, Italy and its antiquities were linked with the earliest recollections of his childhood, and his father was ever urging him to visit the country from which he himself had derived such profit. Once, from the crest of the Alps, Goethe had looked down on its plains, but had been drawn back to Frankfort by Lili Schönemann. He had actually set out in earnest when the messenger of Karl August overtook him with the summons to Weimar. Yet in the years of intense practical activity the dream of Italy had never left him, and he incorporated his longing for the land of his heart's desire in the famous song of Mignon. Finally he had reached a state of mind in which to open a Latin book or to look on a picture of Italy was torment.

What drove Goethe to Italy was primarily the disproportion between his narrow surroundings and the loftiness of his artistic ambitions ; he hoped to find in Italy this disproportion removed in the noble proportions and calm serenity of antique art. For it was primarily as an artist, and not as a poet, that he undertook the journey, and his diaries and letters of this period are almost entirely devoted to descriptions of statues and monuments. Even when he dilates on customs, or landscapes, or poetry, they are considered purely under their plastic aspect. All his life Goethe hovered between the artist and the poet, and while in Italy he had visions of attaining to high excellence in drawing by undergoing a course of intensive training under Tischbein and other German artists in Rome. When not sight-seeing he was sketching, and poetry was relegated to the second place. The 'true art' in which he was to quench his thirst was primarily the classical remains of Rome, and thither he hastened with all speed. Venice completed his alienation from the 'follies' of Gothic art and he left it without reluctance ; he cast but a glance at Florence ; and to the medieval glories of Assisi he obstinately shut his eyes. He reached Rome on October 29, 1786, a date which he came to look upon as his second birthday. Winckelmann's *History of Ancient Art* was his guide, and he spent four months drinking in the manifold impressions of the 'capital of the world.' At the end of February he set out for Naples, still accompanied by Tischbein, and was charmed by its natural beauties ; then on with another artist to Sicily, the 'key of Italy', this being his first sight of the open sea. By June he was back in Rome and, for the last ten months of his stay, made himself thoroughly acquainted with the city, its art, its music and its people. A love affair with a Milanese beauty finally dislodged Frau von Stein from his heart and inspired the charming poem *Cupido, loser, eigensinniger Knabe.* When recalled by the Duke in June 1788 he left Italy with intense regret, but with the feeling that at least he had achieved his aims, that he had cured himself of the physical and moral ills which had tortured him at home, and that the land of art had taught him his true vocation of artist, not, indeed, in the narrow sense of the painter or even the poet, but as the artist of life who aims at developing to the full all the faculties with which he is endowed.

To the student of German literature, however, it is primarily the influence which the Italian journey exercised on his poetry that matters, and on this point critics are not agreed. Though most of them see in the contact with

antique art the completion of his conversion, begun by
Frau von Stein, to noble ideals of moderation and perfect
culture, others consider that his attitude to art was perver-
ted by the notions of pseudo-classicism which he had brought
back with him. The settlement of the dispute will best be
reached by the study of those works inspired by Italy.

Goethe had taken with him to Italy a number of manu-
scripts which he hoped to finish in time for the complete
edition of his works to be published shortly by Göschen. But
the distractions of the stay proved too strong and he only
succeeded in completing *Egmont*, besides adding two scenes
to *Faust*, and recasting the plans of his *Tasso*, and the form
of his *Iphigenie*. *Egmont*, as we have seen, belongs essentially
to the subjective period of the ' Sturm und Drang ', and, but
for the last act, was practically complete. As far as this play
is concerned, the Italian influence was unfortunate : his
sudden interest in Italian opera emphasized the melodramatic
symbolism of the last scene and so destroyed the unity of style.
That he wrote the *Hexenküche* and the *Wald und Höhle* scenes
in *Faust* while in Rome was purely fortuitous, although
critics like to find in Faust's rejuvenation the symbol of his
own spiritual re-birth. *Wilhelm Meister* scarcely progressed
at all, except that he realized more and more that he needed
a broader basis for the education of his hero than the theatrical
world of the *Sendung*. *Iphigenie* on the other hand, though
its conception and poetical elaboration go back to the early
Weimar period, owes much of its present form and spirit
to Italian influences.

What first attracted Goethe in the drama of Euripides was
clearly the analogy of the motif with his own experience ;
in Orestes pursued by the Furies he saw a representation of
himself, tortured as he was by mental distractions and restless
passion. In Iphigenia he saw the personification of his
desires for peace and self-mastery, and in his mind her figure

took on certain characteristics of Frau von Stein, who by her sympathy had done so much to effect his cure. This psychical interpretation of the old myth is far removed, indeed, from the Greek conception of a man, curse-laden by an unjust fate, in tragic conflict with the gods. And so it was that Schiller found the play 'astonishingly modern and un-Greek', and Goethe himself described it as 'devilishly humane', meaning, doubtless, that it was inspired by the ideal of pure humanity which was his gospel of life, as it was that of Lessing, Rousseau, Herder, and of their contemporaries. The idea of abstract truth prevailing over ignorance and barbarity is a conception evolved entirely under the influence of humanitarian enlightenment. *Iphigenie* represents, together with *Nathan der Weise*, the noblest expression of that movement in German literature.

Its pseudo-classical origin is already betrayed by the fact that it was originally planned as a 'Singspiel' or vaudeville, a counterpart to that *Alceste* of Wieland which Goethe had ridiculed so severely a few years before in the farce *Götter, Helden und Wieland* (1774). Two plays of Gotter, his *Orest und Electra* (1772) and *Merope* (1773) (the same Gotter who helped to turn Schiller along the paths of classicism), have also left their mark on *Iphigenie auf Tauris*. In the limitation of the action to a few characters of noble birth, in the simplification of the fable, the close observance of the unities, the high-flown diction, and, above all, in the concentration of the drama in the conflict of soul, *Iphigenie* marks a complete break with the character-tragedy of Shakespeare and a definite return to the tragic ideals of the French 'grand siècle'.

On none of his works did Goethe spend more time filing and polishing than on his *Iphigenie*; written originally in rhythmical prose, it underwent four revisions before being finally cast into its present iambic five-foot lines, under the influence of K. P. Moritz, author and prosodist, the 'dearest associate' of the Roman sojourn. And though the plot and characters remained practically unchanged, yet this transformation of form helped to give *Iphigenie* that sense of elevation, of purity and harmony in language and style, which infuses the whole play with the classical spirit of calm beauty and repose.

Whilst *Iphigenie* can thus be said to possess something of the flavour of Italy, Goethe's next play, *Tasso*, is the very product of the soil. *Tasso*, like *Iphigenie*, was also conceived during the early Weimar years on the basis of personal experience, and the theme is very similar. It also represents the conflict of the ' two souls in the poet's breast ' and the subsequent healing of his mental disease. Tasso, as Goethe himself admitted, has much in common with Werther ; it is the same tragedy of unbalanced ' Schwärmerei ', and in each case the malady is brought to a head by a declaration of love for a woman beyond the hero's reach. But while Werther succumbs to his fate, Tasso is cured, temporarily at least, by the thought of his art :

' Und wenn der Mensch in seiner Qual verstummt,
    Gab mir ein Gott, zu sagen wie ich leide.'

Thus the theme of *Tasso* is, as Goethe once expressed himself to Frau Herder, ' the disproportion between talent and life.' It is the same conflict of the poet wrestling with the realities of life that Grillparzer was to bring to a more fitting tragic issue in *Sappho*. Whether Goethe himself had not originally planned a tragic conclusion for *Tasso*, such as the historical committal to the madhouse, is a mere hypothesis. But this satisfactory conclusion, if ever it existed, was completely modified, as Goethe, under the influence of his Italian experiences, attained to a true knowledge of his real mission in life, that of giving full expression to his personality in his art.

Apart from the main theme, the play owes little enough to Italy. Goethe made no serious study of historical sources; he did not even avail himself of Tasso's correspondence with his patron. The local colour which might have been expected from one familiar with the actual scenes of the drama is almost entirely absent, and there is no attempt to produce the atmosphere of an Italian court of the Renaissance; rather is the background of the play transferred from Ferrara to Weimar, and the Duke transformed into an idealized portrait of Karl August. There has been, however, an undue tendency to look for the originals of the characters of *Tasso* in Goethe's friends and acquaintances at the Weimar court; but while, no doubt, much of Charlotte von Stein, and something of the Duchess Luise of Weimar, has passed into Goethe's Princess, and although a model for Lenore Sanvitale has been found in the Countess von Werthern, these characters owe more to literary tradition. The chief crux in the interpretation of *Tasso* lies, however, in the character of Antonio. As originally conceived, Antonio must have been the prosaic antithesis of Tasso, the representative of the cold, calculating world of fact, jealous of the poet, and plotting his downfall. But in the completed play he is conceived more ideally as the embodiment of a higher practical wisdom, as a rock of strength to which Tasso clings for support. Nor did Goethe really succeed in harmonizing these different conceptions of his character. There is even less action in *Tasso* than in *Iphigenie*, and the tragedy is entirely based on the inner conflict in Tasso's mind. This lack of action is no doubt responsible for the general unpopularity of the drama, but in another sense it marks its importance. Thus *Tasso* looks both backwards and forwards in the development of the European drama; in its spiritualization of the conflict it is reminiscent, as Madame de Staël

pointed out in *De l'Allemagne*, of the tragedy of Racine,
and at the same time it is strangely prophetic of the
modern psychological drama of Hebbel and Ibsen.   Formally
it is the most perfect of Goethe's works ; the harmonious
verse, the restraint of style, the scrupulous observance of the
unities, the well-balanced action and symmetrical relationship of the characters, all confirm Goethe's definite reversion
to the classical drama.

When Goethe returned to Weimar after an absence of
nearly two years he found himself entirely out of touch with
his former surroundings ; he had progressed artistically and
intellectually while his friends had remained at a standstill.
The works into which he had instilled his new ideals, such as
Iphigenie and *Tasso*, were received with cold disapproval by
former admirers.   He also found little sympathy with his
scientific interests ; and the relations with Frau von Stein,
which were already strained at his departure, ended in
a direct breach when he installed in his house a young girl
of the working-classes, Christiane Vulpius, whom he did not
make his wife until eighteen years later.   He had thus
alienated his best friends, and he withdrew into himself.   The
Duke had generously relieved him of most of his duties,
though he continued his salary ; he now enjoyed full leisure
for his avocations, whether scientific or literary.   During the
next few years, until the friendship with Schiller gave new
zest to his literary output, his scientific interests predominated, and he wasted much time combating Newton's
theory of light, or studying the metamorphosis of plants,
valuable time which posterity grudges from his literary
activity.   The chief poetic output of these years is the
Römische Elegien (1795), written under the combined
inspiration of his love for classical antiquity and the new
passion for Christiane.   The naked eroticism of these poems

is typical of the best traditions of Catullus, Tibullus or Propertius ; they are not only classical in form, but pagan in spirit, like no other poems in German literature until we come to Hölderlin, poems frankly delighting in sensuous beauty of love and art. They are immeasurably superior to the political satire and didacticism of the *Epigramme, Venedig 1790*, inspired by a short trip to Venice in that year.

The French Revolution, which had broken out meanwhile, was the occasion of Goethe's accompanying Karl August in the expedition of the Duke of Brunswick against France in 1792, and being present at the Battle of Valmy. He has left a belated record of his impressions—he was much more concerned with his scientific pursuits than with the political and military events of the campaign—in the *Kampagne in Frankreich 1792* (1822). Goethe's attitude to the Revolution was intensely hostile ; his discipline as the servant of the Weimar state, his scientific studies, the serenity of art which he had brought back from Italy, all combined to make him averse to convulsive interruption and lawless change. He first gave literary expression to his political views in some of the *Venetian Epigrams*. These were followed by *Der Grosskophta*, a dramatization of the famous diamond necklace story. *Der Bürgergeneral* is a dramatic jest, but contains nevertheless a lesson of sound practical wisdom for rural Germany, and a word in season to landlords. Goethe's most complete confession of political faith is found in the unfinished drama *Die Aufgeregten*, which was to show how revolutionary outbreaks could best be prevented by correcting abuses in high places. In *Wilhelm Meisters Lehrjahre* we are shown the nobleman Lothario putting these ideals into practice : ' Here or nowhere is America ', he cries. The reformation of our ancient Europe is a nobler task than emigration to a New World. And the marriage of Wilhelm to Nathalie implies

something more than the crowning of a completed apprenticeship ; it is also a symbol of the union of bourgeoisie
and nobility in their common striving for the progress of
humanity.

Whereas the former dramas showed the results, the
symptoms, the frame of mind induced by the Revolution, *Die
natürliche Tochter* (1803) reveals its causes and essential
nature.   Unfortunately, the theoretical and mistaken notions
of dramatic art which underlie the conception of the play
have deprived the theme of any life it might have possessed.
The action is vague, the diction artificial, the characters are
shadowy and unreal.   Far from being a ' lofty and powerful '
embodiment of the greatest political event of modern times,
it is merely the story of a court intrigue, with but the rumble
of revolutionary thunder in the distance.   Goethe failed to
depict the French Revolution worthily, because he had no
sympathy with the abstract principles for which it stood ; he
was hostile to it because it threatened to sink the individual
in the common herd, and to destroy personal culture in favour
of vague and shadowy ideals of equality and fraternity.

VII

GOETHE AND SCHILLER

WHEN Goethe returned from Italy in 1787, it was with a feeling bordering on dismay that he found Schiller established as a literary free-lance in his immediate vicinity. To him Schiller was still the author of *Die Räuber*, the representative of the revolutionary spirit, which was even then threatening to engulf European civilization. Schiller, for his part, was repelled by Goethe's aloofness, and envious of his elder's good fortune ; he was hurt by the coolness of his reception at the hands of the Weimar coterie. Obviously the time was not yet ripe for the literary friendship which is so memorable an event in the history of German letters. Schiller sought solace for his disappointments in work, and turned his attention to history. The first-fruit of his labours was an ambitious *Geschichte des Abfalls der Niederlande* (1788), of which only the first volume ever appeared. This was a period of history which held him as it had once held Goethe, as the embodiment of the glorious struggle for political and intellectual freedom. This work obtained for him, mainly through Goethe's efforts, the appointment to a vacant professorship of History in the University of Jena. His second historical work was the *Geschichte des Dreissigjährigen Krieges* (1791–93), which was intended primarily to provide light reading for the lady readers of Göschen's *Historischer Kalender*. It is obvious that with such an aim the quality of the work could not be very high. History in Schiller's day was not the exact science it became in the nineteenth century under Ranke, but it had certainly advanced further than might be inferred from Schiller's writings. As an historian Schiller completely failed to put into practice, as men like Abbt or Möser had done, the new conception of the evolution of the human race which Herder had taught the world in his *Ideen*. Schiller looked upon history with the eyes of the ' Aufklärer ' ; the philosophical aspect attracted him, and he had a dramatic sense for great characters. Just as he owed much to Voltaire the dramatist, so too he looked up to Voltaire the historian and took from him his broad generalizations, his rhetorical outbursts and fictitious speeches, and, above all, his cosmopolitan outlook. It is not, however, as history that Schiller's historical writings must be judged, but as the creations of a poetical imagination, and it is as such that they occupy a recognized place in German literature.

In 1790 Schiller found complete happiness in his marriage to the gentle Charlotte von Lengefeld—a happiness which was only marred by the constant struggle with illness and his ever-increasing financial difficulties. In 1791 a severe attack completely undermined his health and he lay for some time at the point of death. It was at this moment that help came from a Danish admirer, the Duke of Holstein-Augustenburg, who most opportunely granted him a pension for three years, in order that he might devote himself to his studies free from pecuniary anxieties.

Schiller in the meanwhile had passed from history to philosophy, and, through the advocacy of Körner, had become a warm admirer and adherent of Kant. It was not so much his general principles of philosophy that attracted Schiller as his aesthetic side, and especially the *Kritik der Urteilskraft* (1790), and he gradually devoted all his attention to the narrower field of aesthetics. In the winter of 1792–93 he delivered a course of lectures on this theme : the first positive achieve-

ments of his new interests are embodied in four important
letters written to Körner in 1793, which were prolegomena
to a treatise to be entitled *Kallias oder über die Schönheit*, a
treatise which was never completed.   In these letters he joins
issue with Kant over the definition of beauty : the philosopher denied that there was any objective criterion inherent
in a thing by virtue of which it was beautiful ; Schiller
thought he had discovered such a principle in the illuminating
phrase ' Freiheit in der Erscheinung '.   A work of art was
beautiful when, while it complied with all the requirements
of technique, the laws which conditioned its existence ob-
truded so little on the observer that the object ' appeared '
to be free from constraint, and to be the spontaneous product
of nature.   In his next work, *Über Anmut und Würde* (1793),
Schiller concerns himself with the refutation of Kant's theory
that the highest beauty is incompatible with the human form,
since this can never be dissociated from an intellectual
concept of the moral dignity of human nature.   Schiller tried
to show that there was, apart from what he calls ' archi-
tectonic ' beauty, another beauty in man which has its basis
in the personality : this is ' Anmut ' or Grace and is the
expression of a beautiful personality or of the ' schöne Seele ',
whereas dignity is the expression of a lofty mind.   In the
Briefe über die ästhetische Erziehung des Menschen (1795)
Schiller endeavoured to establish the inseparableness of
beauty and morality which Kant had denied.   It is only the
aesthetic sense that can restore the balance between man's
sensuous and rational nature, and give him that freedom from
the extreme of either emotion which is the basis of true
culture.   This aesthetic faculty which restores the balance of
harmony Schiller designates the ' Play impulse ' (Spieltrieb),
implying by the name that we are thereby restored to the
happy state of children at play.   This ' play impulse ' was

later to influence Friedrich Schlegel in formulating the
famous doctrine of ' romantic irony '.

Thus in philosophy as in history Schiller's works represent
a retrograde movement, a reaction from the ' categorical
imperative ', from the moral faith which requires obedience
freed from all empirical motives and desires, and a movement towards the abstract reason of Enlightenment which
saw the ideal in educating man to the point when he would
will what was right.   In this identification of inclination
and duty Schiller saw the ideal of freedom, an idea which
runs through all his later dramas.

In the treatise *Über naive und sentimentalische Dichtung*
(1795–96) Schiller applied the results of his philosophy to
literature.   Defining as it does his theoretical attitude to
poetry, it deserves more than passing notice.   It is at the same
time the ' art poétique ' of the whole classical period.   What
strikes us most in nature, says Schiller, is its appearance of
simplicity and truth ; in other words, its naïveté, which shows
up the artificiality of our own sentiments.   But this perfection
of natural objects is not their merit, for it is not their choice.
Real perfection consists, as we know, in obeying of one's own
free will the law of necessity ; by willing to attain the perfect
state of natural objects we shall at the same time rise superior
to them.   Now every true genius is naïve or is no genius (such
was the teaching of the ' Sturm und Drang ') : intuitively
needing no rules, yet incapable of going wrong, such are all
great men, whether artists or men of action.   Primitive
peoples living in close touch with nature (e. g. the Greeks)
are naïve.   Our modern civilization, on the other hand, has
left nature behind : whereas the Greeks were themselves
nature, we must seek it outside ourselves ; in other words, we
look upon it ' sentimentally ', as the happy state from which
we departed in the exuberance of our reason.   We regret its

innocence and long for its perfection, and as nature has disappeared from our real, human lives, we look for it in the world of ideas—in poetry.

Now the poets, from the very conception of poetry itself, have always striven to express nature : they either are nature, or they aspire to the nature they have lost ; there are thus two kinds of poets, the naïve and the sentimental. At the dawn of humanity (here the influence of Rousseau is apparent), when man was pure nature, there reigned perfect union of his receptivity and his spontaneity, but with civilization this harmony disappears and, from being real, becomes ideal. The mission of poetry is to be the most complete expression possible of humanity : then the poet who is nature will merely have to express reality; the poet, on the other hand, who is no longer in harmony with nature, must raise reality to the ideal—he is the poet of ideas. Inasmuch as the sentimental poet seeks after the ideal, an infinite conception which can never be attained, he is inferior to the naïve poet, who attains the real, a finite quantity, but he is superior to him as he approaches the supreme goal of humanity, which is the approximation to the infinite.

When a poet opposes reality to the ideal, and insists on the imperfect reality as an object of aversion, then he is satiric ; when on the contrary the poet opposes the ideal to reality, insisting no longer on the real but on the perfection of the ideal, in such a way that it is the pleasure called forth by the ideal which becomes the dominating impression of his work, then he is elegiac. Either he is sad because man has not attained the ideal, and we have the elegy proper, or else nature and the ideal are represented as reached, and we have the idyll. The idyll would thus be the reconciliation of humanity with itself, and as such the idyll represents the highest form of poetic achievement.

Such is the line of argument by which Schiller sought to justify his own type of reflective poetry by the side of that of the ancients and of the naïve poets, and of Goethe particularly.   It is a criticism of poetry based entirely on deductive lines ; there is no attempt to take into consideration, in accordance with Herder's teaching, historical development or national characteristics.   Schiller's standpoint in poetics, as in history and philosophy, is essentially that of eighteenth-century rationalism, and *Über naive und sentimentalische Dichtung* is really but another belated engagement in the battle of the Ancients and Moderns, in which the victory is apportioned to neither side.   But Schiller's criticism was not merely negative, it was also constructive : in the distinction he drew between naïve and sentimental, he anticipated and prepared for the critical theories of Friedrich Schlegel, who learned from Schiller to oppose ancient to modern poetry, objective to subjective poetry, or, to use his particular terminology, classical to romantic poetry.

As Goethe pointed out to Eckermann many years later, *Über naive und sentimentalische Dichtung* was undertaken by Schiller with the definite object of justifying his own art by the side of Goethe's.   When he had determined that there was room in the world for his 'sentimental' poetry as well as for Goethe's 'naïve' art, there was no further obstacle to an understanding between the two poets.   Goethe for his part was agreeably surprised by the objectivity of a review of *Egmont* which Schiller had written in 1788, and the poem *Die Götter Griechenlands* (1788) had taught him that Schiller's appreciation of the Greek genius was not, after all, so much less than his own.   And so, when in 1794 Schiller wrote to invite his collaboration in a new journal *Die Horen* (1795–97), Goethe readily accepted.   A chance conversation with Schiller shortly afterwards concerning his hobby, the meta-

morphosis of plants, convinced him that, if as a critic he
could not always see eye to eye with him, yet he was no
unworthy opponent. From this date until Schiller's death in
1805 a correspondence passed between the two poets, which
is an invaluable commentary on the ideals and achievements
of the classical period, while the letters themselves are
masterpieces of German prose. Schiller's famous *aperçu* of
Goethe's creative powers contained in the letter of August 23,
1794, still affords the most illuminating insight into a poet's
mind ever written ; it did much to confirm Goethe in his
belief that he had at last found no mere laudatory admirer,
but a critic with a sympathetic understanding of his personality.
'You sum up my existence', answered Goethe, expressing
the hope that they would henceforth be able to strive after
a common ideal. Schiller replied on August 31 with another
letter, in which he drew the same clear picture of his own
intellectual nature, and at the same time pointed out the
divergences of their interests, and of their respective creative
talent. It was a subject which, as we have seen, had occupied
his mind deeply during the work on *Über naive und sentimentalische Dichtung*, and he was convinced that Goethe was the
realist, the naïve poet *per se*, while he himself was the idealist,
the sentimental poet. The importance of the literary friendship lies in this very fact, that Schiller led Goethe to look
within, to consider the inward significance of his works ;
Schiller on the other hand learnt from Goethe to look to the
real world without, to pay attention to details. They thus
in a large measure completed each other. But we must
beware of over-estimating the influence of the two poets upon
each other ; the terms of friendship were not quite equal.
Schiller looked up to his brother-poet with a certain reverence
which Goethe accepted as his due, and whereas he submitted
his plans, and even his works, for Goethe's criticism, and acted

upon it, Goethe, on his side, was much less communicative, and rarely asked Schiller's advice. But for both the union acted as an intellectual stimulus, as a quickening of their poetic powers, and it was in this sense that Goethe could refer to the period as a ' second spring '.

The first product of the intimacy of the two poets was *Wilhelm Meisters Lehrjahre*, which Goethe was then completing, and Schiller's letters are filled with criticisms and appreciations of the novel. Goethe had profoundly modified the plan of the work as we know it in the *Theatralische Sendung*. The manifold experiences he had undergone in the meanwhile have left their mark on the new conception of the novel. The first six books are in essence the same apprenticeship to the theatre which was the subject of the *Sendung*, but in the last three we are transported into the artificial world of secret brotherhoods and mystifications. These have their origin in the rage of the time for freemasonry and secret societies, of which the ' Illuminati ' of Weisshaupt are the chief example. Wilhelm is initiated into the mysteries, only to learn that the true philosophy of life is ' to live '. Not that the motif appears at all clearly in the work : it is overwhelmed by the mass of irrelevant padding of which the pietistic *Bekenntnisse einer schönen Seele* is the most out-of-place. It is especially this confusion of ideas, this complete disregard of artistic composition, that makes *Wilhelm Meister* the most unsatisfactory of Goethe's works, and the modern reader gladly turns from its incoherence to the living interest and spontaneity of the *Theatralische Sendung*, which contains all that is memorable in the *Lehrjahre*, without its obscurity. Schiller was nevertheless disappointed not to receive the *Lehrjahre* for his *Horen* ; instead Goethe sent him the *Unterhaltungen deutscher Ausgewanderten* (1795), mostly trivial tales retold from the French, and devoid of poetic value. At the end of the collection is the *Märchen*, an incomprehensible phantasmagoria after the manner of the mystifications of *Wilhelm Meister*, for which Carlyle, with all his enthusiasm, failed to find a satisfactory interpretation. From the literary point of view, Goethe's *Märchen* was the forerunner of similar fantastic tales of the Romantic School.

Even apart from these tales Goethe's other contributions to the *Horen* were not calculated to make the new periodical a success : the *Römische Elegien* caused offence by their frank sensuality ; the translation of the autobiography of Benvenuto Cellini was, after all, but a translation. Nor were Schiller's profound *Briefe über die ästhetische Erziehung des Menschen*, or a purely historical sketch like the *Belagerung von Antwerpen*, likely to prove much more acceptable to the reading public. But though the two poets had only themselves to blame, they yet felt deeply aggrieved by the failure of the journal, Goethe in particular being stung by the neglect with which his scientific works were treated by the scientists of the day, while Schiller was annoyed by the lack of recognition given to his aesthetic studies. At Goethe's suggestion the poets retaliated with the *Xenien*, epigrammatic couplets in the style of Martial's *Xenia*, which appeared in the new *Musenalmanach* for 1796. They were directed mainly against the littérateurs and journalists of the day : Nicolai, Lavater, the Stolbergs, Lichtenberg, Jung Stilling, came in for a severe drubbing ; others like Herder and Wieland received only a little harmless chaff. It is difficult to understand the flutter which these 'little fellows' caused among the literary dovecots of the day : once deprived of their personalities they contain but little real sting. Nor did they pass unchallenged, for the victims rounded on the attackers with a virulence which equalled, if it did not excel, the efforts of the two friends. In any case the results were purely negative, as Goethe and Schiller themselves soon came to see. ' After the mad venture of the *Xenien* we must devote ourselves to great and worthy works of art,' wrote Goethe in November 1796. The positive expression of this conviction was *Hermann und Dorothea* and *Wallenstein*.

In the meanwhile, as a kind of interlude, came the ' Balladenjahr' of 1797, which brought a new and wonderful harvest. Goethe had for years had many ballad-subjects at hand which were only waiting for the inspiration of the moment. Schiller had always felt attracted by the half-epic, half-lyric genre. This interest in ballad poetry was more the direct outcome of their friendship than any other of their poetic creations. They chose their subjects together, and discussed them in their letters. Schiller especially, as in the case of the *Kraniche des Ibykus*, often submitted his poems for his friend's criticism and followed his suggestions without question. Schiller opened the series with *Der Taucher*; then followed *Der Handschuh, Der Ring des Polykrates, Der Ritter Toggenburg, Die Kraniche des Ibykus, Der Gang nach dem Eisenhammer, Der Kampf mit dem Drachen, Die Bürgschaft.* To these were added in later years *Der Graf von Habsburg, Hero und Leander,* and *Kassandra.* Goethe composed his *Zauberlehrling, Die Braut von Korinth, Gott und die Bajadere* and the cycle of *Die schöne Müllerin,* all works reminiscent in their directness and spontaneity of the poetry of his early days. But while for Goethe the ballad seemed the legitimate form for expressing the mysterious forces and feelings of the human heart, as represented by ancient myths and legends, to Schiller it was another vehicle for inculcating moral principles. Goethe's ballads recall the world of ' fog and mist' of his early poetry ; Schiller's are imaginative reflective poems with a philosophical background. They are, as Schiller wrote to Goethe, ' the embodiment of

ideas ' ; in one case the motif is provided by the notion of
an avenging nemesis, in another by the moral majesty of self-
conquest, in yet another it is the triumph of friendship or love
true to death. Nor can all the splendour of description, the
stirring dramatic situation, the dignified and classical language
make up for the lack of that naïveté and sincerity which
characterizes Goethe's ballads. Yet, despite the critic,
Schiller's ballads, perhaps even because of that mild didacticism which makes them inferior as works of art, are
greater favourites with the German people than Goethe's.

The extent to which Schiller's ballads partake of the
philosophic lyric is shown by *Das Eleusische Fest*, which
treats in the ballad metre of the beginnings of civilization, just
as earlier *Die Künstler* had dealt with the humanizing of man.
Such metrical rhetoric is one of Schiller's great sources of
poetic strength ; he reaches supreme excellence in the
' lyric of ideas ' which he had cultivated already with such
success in *Die Götter Griechenlands* (1788) and *Die Künstler*
(1789). While the theme of both these poems is of art as
the great teacher and refiner of mankind, the great poems of
the period of his friendship with Goethe are the quintessence
of the ripe philosophic thought to which Schiller had attained
under the inspiration of Kant. *Die Ideale* is Schiller's farewell
to the flaccid sentimentality of his youth and contains a
stimulating gospel of work. In a poem like *Das Ideal und das
Leben*, unequalled of its kind, Schiller has expressed poetically
his ideal creed, the belief that man can only obtain perfect peace and happiness by escaping from the bondage of
the senses into the realm of the ideal. *Der Genius* was
inspired by Goethe, the naïve genius in whom Schiller revered
the essence of the poetic spirit. *Die Würde der Frauen* is
a panegyric of women as the healers and guardian angels of
men, and is written under the inspiration of the ' ideal '

woman, Schiller's wife. *Der Spaziergang* is the culmination of Schiller's philosophic lyric, in which, true to the precepts of the *Laokoon*, description is translated into movement. Round a walk into the country the poet has woven a loving contemplation of nature seen in its relation to the development of human life in accordance with Herder's *Ideen*. Schiller liked to consider this poem, standing as it does half-way between the elegy and the idyll, as the most perfect of his creations. Posterity has, however, given the palm to *Das Lied von der Glocke* (1799) which is both more plastic and less abstruse than *Der Spaziergang*. No philosophic training is needed to understand and enjoy this poem. In the founding of the bell Schiller has symbolized the various phases of the human life ; its sound accompanies man from his baptism to his burial. The freshness of the poem has been weakened by constant repetition, but its popularity is explained by the way it transmutes the commonplace metal of everyday life into the gold of poetry. It thus belongs to the same homely world of German national life as *Hermann und Dorothea*.

In their correspondence the two poets discuss at some length the theory of epic poetry. Both of them in subsequent years planned epics on various subjects, and *Hermann und Dorothea* is more the direct result of the ' second spring-tide ', which the friendship with Schiller produced, than any other of Goethe's works. The execution of the *bürgerliches Idyll* went on in Jena, almost under Schiller's eyes, with extraordinary facility and rapidity. Within nine days the first four cantos were complete, and every evening the daily portion was read to Schiller and his wife. But when Goethe was once back amid the distraction and bustling life of Weimar the work came to a standstill, and was not actually finished until the middle of 1797, after Wilhelm von Humboldt had assisted in the revision of the metre. It is probably to this unusual

rapidity of composition that the poem owes its perfection
of form.

Goethe had a model in the *Luise* of Voss, which he had
always admired and much of which he knew by heart, and
from *Luise* he has borrowed something of the setting and the
metre.   But while Voss was content to depict faithfully and
accurately real, simple, genial persons, and the smallest
particulars of reality, Goethe has raised his characters into
universal types of human existence, and invested his descriptions with movement.

This classicism of *Hermann und Dorothea* is at once its
weakness and its greatness.   Goethe does not present us, as
some critics would have us believe, with a realistic picture of
German middle-class life as it was, but as he saw it through the
idealized spectacles of his classical outlook.   It is not, however,
the spirit of Homer which inspires the poem—the disproportion between the homely subject and the heroic style is on
occasion almost ludicrous—but that of a theoretical classicism.
True to the eighteenth-century conception of classical art
Goethe has endeavoured to attain to its supposed ideality and
repose by eliminating crude reality and individual character.
It is the abstract conceptions for which his characters stand
that interest Goethe most.   Hermann is the ideal of a simple,
shy German youth, as opposed to Dorothea's first lover, who,
enthusiastic visionary that he was, died fighting for the
revolution.   Dorothea is the typical German maiden whose
mission in life is to be half-wife, half-servant to her lord :
' Dienen lerne bei Zeiten das Weib nach ihrer Bestimmung '.
Even the Apotheker is typically conceived.   Yet Goethe's
innate realism saved his work from lifelessness and dullness.
He is not even afraid of trivialities, if they but serve to
visualize an event or an object, and so many little details concerning the scene of the action are woven into the narrative

that it is quite possible to reconstruct the little Rhine town and its setting of hills and vineyards with considerable accuracy. The incidents which he describes are typical scenes taken straight from German life, such as that of the well, where Hermann finds Dorothea, but dare not open his heart to her. It is such passages of naïveté and tenderness, in which the poem abounds, that have made *Hermann und Dorothea* popular with the general reading public of Germany. But even a consummate artist like Platen, though he censured the ruggedness of the hexameters, could admire the poem as the 'pride of Germany and the pearl of art'.

Schiller's positive achievement after the 'Xenienkampf' was the tragedy of *Wallenstein*. He was encouraged by Goethe's interest, and the play which had been germinating in his mind since 1791 began to take definite form. In the ten years which lay between the publication of *Don Carlos* and the completion of *Wallenstein* the intensive training in history and philosophy Schiller had undergone had broadened his outlook on life and art. But he was still convinced that the dramatic path which he had followed in *Don Carlos* was the right one, and Goethe's example and influence only served to confirm him in this belief. The advance which doubtless is present in *Wallenstein* is due chiefly to the substitution of Greek for the French models of *Don Carlos*. In preparation Schiller steeped himself in the *Poetics* of Aristotle, he read the *Philoktetes*, *The Trojan Women* of Euripides, and *Œdipus Rex* of Sophocles. He thought he discovered in the Wallenstein story a motif similar to *Œdipus*, that of a man in the grip of an adverse fate. But Wallenstein's belief in astrology is not the symbol of an overruling destiny, even though the poet ascribes 'the greater half of his guilt to his unlucky stars'. Wallenstein's fate rests all the time in his own hands : thus it is his final decision to join the Swedes which induces Piccolomini to act. Schiller's view of fate was not that of the Greeks : he was far too much a child of the ' Aufklärung' to believe in such 'grotesque rubbish', and it was only Goethe's approval which induced him to retain the astrological motive he found in his sources and lend it such prominence.   He had learned from Kant to consider every human action as a link in the chain of natural causes.   While in the world of phenomena there was thus no escape from determinism, Kant postulated a moral world in which man retained his freedom of will.   An act might therefore be strictly determined in time and space, and yet, at the same time, be free in the intelligible world of ultimate reality.   It is in this sense that Wallenstein, though all his acts are carefully conditioned by others which have preceded them, compasses his destruction through his own guilt. ' In deiner Brust sind deines Schicksals Sterne,' says Illo to him.   There can be no question of *Wallenstein* being a ' Fate Drama ' in the Greek sense, in the way that later the *Braut von Messina* aspired to be. From *Œdipus Rex*, however, Schiller learned the method of ' tragic analysis '.   To the Greek drama he owes the masterly presentation of the pressure of external circumstances which eventually force the decision.

Chief among the influences which went to the making of *Wallenstein* was Schiller's renewed interest in Shakespeare. In *Macbeth* especially he saw obvious points of contact with his own fable.   It is significant that, soon after the completion of *Wallenstein*, Schiller actually adapted *Macbeth* for the Weimar stage, and there is no better example by which to illustrate the diametrically opposed methods of the two dramatists.   While Shakespeare was content to represent the story as a piece of life, as the great natural tragedy of overweening ambition, Schiller considered it in its moral aspect, and made the hero's fall the just retribution for his transgression of the

moral law. Schiller misunderstood Shakespeare, and read
into him his own Kantian theory that the things of this
earth are but the counterpart of a higher world order.
Shakespeare's theme is the fullness of human life ; Schiller's
the moral that can be read into life.

It is obvious that under these conditions *Wallenstein* could
not owe much to Macbeth, or, indeed, to any Shakespearian
character. Schiller had no understanding for a type of evil
however magnificent in itself, and he deemed it necessary to
cast about for a means to idealize his hero's character, to
palliate his crime, in order, as he thought, the better to arouse
the tragic sympathy of the spectator. But Wallenstein was
too essentially the realist : ' His character is never noble and
may not be so,' wrote Schiller himself, and he gave up the
task as impossible. The sympathy which he found himself
unable to bestow on his hero—he confessed to Goethe
that he had never experienced such coolness towards
his theme—he sought as a true Kantian in the pair of
' beautiful souls ', Max and Thekla. He infused them with
the idealism in which his chief character was deficient and
without which the representation of human life would be
imperfect. This introduction of the two lovers out of
deference to his aesthetic theories—Max has no counterpart
in history—no doubt explains their artificiality and unreality.
Max is almost too abstract a conception to be imagined as real
flesh and blood. The conflict in Max's soul between his
inclination and his duty savours too much of an illustration
to a philosophical thesis. Nor is Thekla drawn with any
very clear strokes ; she is scarcely the ' starkes Mädchen '
one would expect Wallenstein's daughter to be. In introducing the love episodes Schiller was not only satisfying his
own desires for an idyllic situation in the midst of the realistic
horrors of war, but was also making a concession to the taste

of the day, which was still under the spell of French tragedy with its 'noble et belle passion'. But, however incongruously the episode strikes the modern critic, it aroused immense enthusiasm among Schiller's contemporaries, when at the time of the War of Liberation every volunteer imagined himself a Max Piccolomini.

In outward form *Wallenstein* is one long drama in ten acts preceded by a one-act play, *Wallensteins Lager*, which is distinguished from the tragedy by a difference of language and rhy.hm. Criticism can find little fault with the vivid presentation of the types of soldiers which make up Wallenstein's heterogeneous army. The same may be said of the figure of the Capuchin monk in the *Lager*, a near relation of the Pater of *Die Räuber*, who preaches his inimitable sermon with extraordinary effect. And the famous song which the Wallensteiners sing, 'Wohl auf, Kameraden, aufs Pferd, aufs Pferd !' was the starting-point for all the lyric poetry of the 'Befreiungskrieg', from which Schenkendorf, Arndt, and Theodor Körner (who could recite the whole *Lager* by heart !) drew their inspiration.

All Schiller's dramas hitherto, even *Wallenstein*, had dealt with the contrast of the real and the ideal ; in his next play, *Maria Stuart* (1800), there is little external conflict. What obviously attracted Schiller in the historical character of the Scottish Queen was not the struggle with a political rival and her subsequent sacrifice to the public weal—it was rather the essentially human interest of Mary's sufferings. The conflict from being external has become inward and spiritual : it is between her physical and her spiritual nature. She is still attached to the world by ties of state policy and especially by her love for Leicester, and to regain her freedom and enjoy her life she is ready (like any of Hebbel's heroines) to make every sacrifice save that of her personality. In the famous confrontation with Elizabeth in the third act, her outraged womanhood rises in revolt ; she answers scorn with scorn and spiritually her rival is entirely routed. Though she goes forth as victor from the encounter, her fate is now sealed; but she is resigned to her lot, and has learnt to look upon it as a just penance for the sins of her passionate nature. By this voluntary resignation to her fate, by thus willing her own death, she fulfils the law of freedom in unity with necessity, which according to Schiller (and Kant) is the ideal of humanity.

In order to fit in the characters with his preconceived scheme Schiller was obliged to take great liberty with them and especially with that of Elizabeth. The ' good Queen Bess ' of English history he has turned into a jealous shrew, who might have stepped straight out of a comedy of intrigue. It is no doubt this travesty of history that renders the play unacceptable to English readers, and the opposite reason helps to explain some of its vogue on the Continent, especially in France, where through the enthusiastic advocacy of Madame de Staël it soon became popular. The intrigue, the motif of the man between two women, the relative observance of the unities (the action is concentrated within three days), the presentation on the stage of the dénouement alone, and, above all, the culmination of the drama in the inward and spiritual conflict, all these go to make a tragedy on the lines of French classicism.

After considering many plans for a new drama, among others one on Perkin Warbeck, Schiller finally decided in favour of *Die Jungfrau von Orleans* (1801). The absolute disregard of historical truth which jarred on the reader in *Maria Stuart* is here still more pronounced ; it is difficult to accept the fiction which makes the poor martyr of Rouen die a glorious death on the battlefield, merely that the dénouement may fit in with Schiller's theory of tragedy. For in *Die Jungfrau von Orleans*, as in all Schiller's plays since *Don Carlos*, the motif is that of human inclination in conflict with the moral law ; in *Die Jungfrau* it is that of her love in collision with the duty to her mission that is the undoing of the maid, and it is only by renouncing her love that she can undergo a moral regeneration in death. Under the influence of the Romantic School then rising into prominence, Schiller entitled his play 'eine romantische Tragödie'. Tieck claimed that it was actually inspired by his *Genoveva*, but it is only the purely external paraphernalia of dreams and visions that Schiller has taken over from Romanticism. He was far too classical in sympathy ever to have approached that negation of form which is the characteristic and, at the same time, the weakness of the Romantic drama. Indeed, in spite of its external appearance of Romanticism, *Die Jungfrau von Orleans* is of all his dramas the most harmoniously classical in style. In some respects, in the battle scenes for instance, it is reminiscent of Shakespearian technique, but Schiller's essentially reflective, ' sentimental ' art has not succeeded here, any more than in *Wallenstein*, in calling up a worthy realistic background for the great clash of political and national rivalries that was the Hundred Years War.

Of all the last great dramas of Schiller, all but one are on historical subjects : *Die Braut von Messina* he declared to be entirely his own invention. Although not based on historical fact, the fable of this play is made up of motifs which were very much in vogue in eighteenth-century literature. The hatred of two brothers and their love for the same woman Schiller had actually treated himself in *Die Räuber*. But while the subject-matter can thus scarcely be termed original, the form is entirely his own. He was actuated by a desire to compete with the Greeks on their own ground, but failed because he did not proceed radically enough. The weakness of the tragedy lies in the fact that it is neither entirely Greek, nor entirely modern ; it is not consistent, for instance, in creating purely passive figures, whose actions are merely the effect of a malignant fate. On the contrary, it is Don Cesar's violence of temperament which is chiefly responsible for the tragedy, while his suicide is in accordance with Schiller's favourite doctrine of the voluntary fulfilment of the moral law. There is in the play much more of the spirit of Corneille's *Rodogune* than of *Œdipus Rex*. Many of the sentiments are incongruously modern, and even the form, in spite of its extreme simplicity, is not Greek. There is in Greek tragedy no instance of a chorus being divided against itself in two hostile camps. None of Schiller's dramas, moreover, makes the same impression of artificiality as *Die Braut von Messina* does. It is less strict necessity than chance that rules in the drama, and there would be no tragedy but for the complaisance of the queen-mother in withholding, at the critical moment, the obvious information as to her daughter's place of refuge. In this sense, at least, it was an undoubted forerunner of the 'Schicksalstragödie', where the same blind fate brings the characters into the most unlikely situations. When the worst has been said, however, *Die Braut von Messina* yet remains a magnificent experiment, and an eloquent testimony to the versatility of Schiller's genius, while the reflective effusions of the chorus are amongst the most touching and beautiful examples of his philosophic poetry.

In contrast to the freely imagined plot of *Die Braut von Messina* he returned in the last drama to be completed to an historical source (or to one that long passed as such), that of Wilhelm Tell. *Tell* is the most popular of Schiller's dramas and has been accounted by many as his greatest work. For one who had to draw his information from books and atlases, the local colouring is strikingly accurate and we have it on the authority of the realist, Gottfried Keller, that his pictures of the Swiss people are true to nature, in spite of their obvious idealization. In this respect Shakespeare's *Julius Caesar*, which had just appeared on the Weimar boards in Schlegel's masterly translation, has left its mark. There breathes over the whole drama an air of freshness and sincerity which at times reminds one of Goethe. There is a breadth of treatment in the succession of idyllic tableaux and plastic details that is rather epic than dramatic. Indeed, Goethe with truer poetic insight had long planned an epic on Tell, when he made over the theme to his friend. The character of Tell, as Schiller conceived it, does not lend itself to dramatic treatment ; he has none of the human faults and frailties of the dramatic hero. He is so idealized as an immaculate type, that even his unheroic murder of Gessler and the cruel rejection of the Parricida are presented as acts deserving of praise rather than of moral censure. Indeed the sententiousness of Tell and his eternal self-consciousness are unendurable, and destroy all sympathy for him as a man. Nor is he even the typical representative of his fellow-countrymen; he refuses to take part in the conspiracy against the existing government until he is personally outraged by the tyrant. It would be difficult to see why he appealed to the Germans as the embodiment of patriotic fervour, were it not for the spirited maxims with which the play abounds : ' Wir wollen sein ein einzig Volk von Brüdern ' and ' Ans Vaterland, ans teure schliess' dich an ! ' During the time of the War of Liberation from Napoleon the Germans saw in the uprising of the Swiss against their Austrian oppressors a symbol of their own struggle for freedom and independence against the tyranny of the French.

It appears doubtful whether in his last tragedy of *Demetrius*

Schiller would have succeeded any better in developing a
national German drama than he had done hitherto. But there
was at least in the story of the Russian pretender the germ of
a psychological problem such as actually did appeal to Hebbel :
that of a man who, though he has lost faith in his own cause, is
bound to carry on the deceit for the sake of those who still
believe in him. But here again Schiller wavered tentatively
between two conceptions of the drama : in the magnificent
scene in the Polish Diet he approaches to the grand historical
background of Shakespeare ; in the problem of Demetrius'
conscious deceit he was once again enthralled by the problem
of man in conflict with the moral law. To what extent he
might have found a harmonious solution in *Demetrius* must
ever remain a matter of doubt, for the play is a torso. But
it would appear extremely doubtful if here, any more than in
his previous dramas, he would have emancipated himself from
that conception of ' the drama considered as a moral institution' which pervades the whole series of his plays from *Die
Räuber* to *Wilhelm Tell*. It is only the different aspects of the
moral law which vary as time goes on. Under the influence
of Rousseau, Schiller is obsessed by the idea of freedom and
duty in their various relations to society. We have the
criticism of reality in *Die Räuber*, *Fiesco*, and *Kabale und
Liebe*. Under the influence of Kant and the humanizing
tendencies of a settled career, of marriage, and especially of
Goethe, the conflict from being external became inward'
and spiritual. Schiller no longer measures reality by the
absolute, but seeks rather to represent the ideal. Beginning
with *Don Carlos*, which marks the transition between
the two conceptions (as it also marks the change of style),
we have a series of noble or tragic characters (Wallenstein, Maria Stuart, Don Cesar, Die Jungfrau von Orleans,
Wilhelm Tell), who, in one way or another, are brought into

direct conflict with the moral law, and either find spiritual
regeneration in the voluntary fulfilment of it, or are crushed
by its negation. And as, to represent the ideal, he needed
nobler material than he found in real life, Schiller was forced
to idealize his characters beyond measure. Hence his continual
travesty of history, which he regards as a convenient store-house
of illustrations for his theories. Hence also his sympathy for
the idealized type of the French classical drama, with its moral
crises, and its lofty rhetoric and pathetic declamation.

Like every great dramatist Schiller was attracted by the
supreme greatness of Shakespeare, but he read into him his
own conception of the universe ; he falsely imagined each of
Shakespeare's plays to be a trial of good and evil before the
judgement-seat of morality. What interested him was not
so much the English poet's great characters in themselves as
their actions in relation to that higher moral law which under-
lies his whole conception of human life. Hence it is that
Schiller's creations lack the spontaneity of natural beings ;
they exist only in so far as they bear some relation to the moral
law which they are about to transgress or fulfil, and their
actions, or rather the attitudes they strike, are conditioned
entirely by this abstract conception, like marionettes by a wire.
If in spite of these drawbacks they still seem alive, it is solely
because Schiller has breathed into them his own great moral
soul, the fire and pathos of his poetry.

Through Schiller the moral and aesthetic world-order,
which had hitherto been a mere tool of rationalism, became
infused with a new life, and its consequences are felt down to
the present day. The whole idealistic tendencies of German
culture, such interests as exist amongst the larger public for
aesthetic or moral questions, for intellectual problems and
abstract concepts of fatherland, freedom, nature, virtue,
friendship, have all been disseminated by the popularity

of Schiller's dramas. To the German public, brought up as it is on Schiller at school, he is still *the* poet, while Goethe stands aloof on Olympian heights. And it would seem as if the German people in their present calamities were once more turning to Schiller's idealistic fervour for consolation and strength. They are learning from him anew the lessons of devotion to duty and subordination of the individual to the common weal.

But great as is his importance as a formative impulse, his influence on the development of the German drama was negative and retrograde. Such poets as followed in his footsteps, Körner, Uhland, Wildenbruch, merely imitated his rhetoric without catching his fire, and modern German drama has developed on very different lines. Inasmuch, however, as the form and contents of his plays won over the general public to the greater appreciation of the grand historical drama, and especially of Shakespeare, and awakened its interest in spiritual problems, he is one of the chief founders of the national German theatre.

During the whole of the nineteenth century we have the curious situation of a poet whose aesthetic and artistic ideals are essentially those of the cosmopolitan eighteenth century held up in Germany as the great national poet, whereas, except amongst intellectuals, Goethe is relegated to the second place. The exaltation of Schiller to the detriment of Goethe was especially marked during the centenary celebrations of the poet's birth in 1859. But this is a point of view to which the literary and critical world (even in Germany) has never subscribed. In this respect it is instructive to note the less emotional and more scientific attitude reflected in the innumerable critical appreciations of the poet which appeared at the centenary of the poet's death in 1905. It is frankly recognized that much of Schiller belongs to the past, that intellectually he is no innovator, but stands deeply indebted to Kant, Rousseau, Goethe, Shakespeare ; that his importance is not as a creative genius but as the disseminator of intellectual concepts. But although as a poet, as a creative artist, he cannot compare with Goethe, yet as a dramatist, as a rhetorician, as an apostle, he is his superior. And his incomparably greater influence upon the German people comes from the unique combination of these qualities in the same person.

Goethe felt the loss of Schiller very deeply ; it was, he said, as though he had lost half his life. Though he lived for another twenty-seven years, he never surpassed, or even approached, the works of his early life and of the period of friendship with Schiller. His later years are devoted essentially to putting into practice the theory of individual life he had indicated in *Wilhelm Meister* : to express his personality to the utmost of his power. For Goethe is a world in himself, sufficient unto himself, answering to no laws except those of his own nature, the greatest creative genius since Shakespeare. And inasmuch as he was conscious of this development towards ever greater perfection, as every step represented a new struggle to a completer, fuller, richer life, and resulted in the feeling of responsibility to himself and his ideals, he is at the same time one of the greatest teachers and educators of the human race. In his striving for completeness he attracted the whole of life within his orbit ; in the breadth of his outlook he is only comparable to the greatest thinkers and artists of ancient Greece.

SELECT BIBLIOGRAPHY

CHAPTERS I and II and GENERAL

H. Hettner, *Geschichte der deutschen Literatur im 18. Jahrhundert,* Braunschweig, 1923[7].

W. Scherer, *Geschichte der deutschen Literatur,* Berlin, 1921[15].

F. Vogt und M. Koch, *Geschichte der deutschen Literatur,* Leipzig, 1922[4].

A. Biese, *Deutsche Literaturgeschichte,* München, 1920[16].

R. M. Meyer, *Die deutsche Literatur bis zum Beginn des 19. Jahrhunderts,* Berlin, 1920[2].

F. J. Schneider, *Die deutsche Dichtung vom Ausgang des Barocks bis zum Beginn des Klassizismus, 1700–1785,* Stuttgart, 1924.

A. Köster, *Die deutsche Literatur der Aufklärungszeit,* Heidelberg, 1925.

K. Lamprecht, *Deutsche Geschichte,* viii. Band, erste Hälfte. Berlin, 1921[4]. *Zeitalter des subjektiven Seelenlebens.*

A. Bossert, *Histoire de la littérature allemande,* Paris, 1913[4].

A. Chuquet, *Études de littérature allemande,* Paris, 1900–2.

L. Reynaud, *L'influence française en Allemagne,* Paris, 1915[2].

K. Francke, *History of German Literature as determined by Social Forces,* London, 1909[3].

C. Thomas, *History of German Literature,* New York, 1909.

J. G. Robertson, *A History of German Literature,* Edinburgh, 1902.

L. M. Price, *English-German Literary Influences,* University of California Publications, 1920, vol. ix.

G. Belouin, *De Gottsched à Lessing,* Paris, 1909.

F. Gundolf, *Shakespeare und der deutsche Geist,* Berlin, 1914[2].

CHAPTER III

E. Schmidt, *Lessing,* Berlin, 1884.

K. Borinsky, *Lessing,* Berlin, 1900.

W. Oehlke, *Lessing und seine Zeit,* München, 1919.

W. Dilthey, *Das Erlebnis und die Dichtung,* Leipzig, 1921[7]. Chapters I–V.

G. Kettner, *Lessings Dramen im Lichte ihrer und unserer Zeit,* Berlin, 1907.

J. Sime, *Lessing, His Life and Works,* London, 1877.

CHAPTER IV

R. Unger, *Hamann und die Aufklärung*, Jena, 1911.
R. Bürkner, *Herder, sein Leben und sein Wirken*, Berlin, 1904.
E. Kühnemann, *Herder*, München, 1912².
A. Bossert, *Herder*, Paris, 1916.
G. P. Gooch, *Germany and the French Revolution*, London, 1920.

CHAPTERS V and VI

H. A. Korff, *Geist der Goethezeit*, I. Teil: *Sturm und Drang*, Leipzig, 1923.
G. H. Lewes, *The Life of Goethe*, London, 1855.
P. Hume Brown, *Life of Goethe*, London, 1920.
J. G. Robertson, *Goethe in the Twentieth Century*, Cambridge, 1912.
H. Loiseau, *L'Évolution morale de Gœthe*, Paris, 1911;
A. Bielschowsky, *Goethe*, München, 1919³⁶.
R. M. Meyer, *Goethe*, Berlin, 1913.
F. Gundolf, *Goethe*, Berlin, 1920.
E. Ludwig, *Goethe*, Stuttgart, 1924².
Benedetto Croce, *Goethe*, English Translation, London, 1923.
W. Rose, *From Goethe to Byron, The Development of 'Weltschmerz' in German Literature*, London, 1924.
A. Kontz, *Les Drames de la Jeunesse de Schiller*, Paris, 1899.

CHAPTER VII

O. Harnack, *Schiller*, Berlin, 1905³.
E. Kühnemann, *Schiller*, München, 1920⁶.
K. Berger, *Schiller*, München, 1920¹².
L. Bellermann, *Schillers Dramen*, Berlin, 1919⁴–1920⁵.
T. Carlyle, *Life of Schiller*, 1825.
H. W. Nevinson, *Life and Writings of Frederick Schiller*, London, 1889.
C. Thomas, *The Life and Works of Frederick Schiller*, New York, 1906.
V. Basch, *La Poétique de Schiller*, Paris, 1911².
J. G. Robertson, *Schiller after a Century*, Edinburgh, 1905.
A. Ludwig, *Schiller und die deutsche Nachwelt*, Berlin, 1909.

INDEX

DATE

MAY 2 4 1977	
MAR 2 4 1982	
JA 26 '87	
GAYLORD	